To Jennifer,

In grateful
appreciation of your contribution to
this publication — the visual
creation of my three poetic symbols:
Jester, demon & puppet.

Sincerely.

Sandra.

PIAVE, BOITO, PIRANDELLO–
FROM ROMANTIC REALISM TO MODERNISM

PIAVE, BOITO, PIRANDELLO–
FROM ROMANTIC REALISM TO MODERNISM

Deirdre O'Grady

Studies in Italian Literature
Volume 10

The Edwin Mellen Press
Lewiston•Queenston•Lampeter

Library of Congress Cataloging-in-Publication Data

  Piave, Boito, Pirandello – From Romantic Realism to Modernism /
Deirdre O'Grady.

ISBN 0-7734-7703-9   (hard)

This is volume 10 in the continuing series
Studies in Italian Literature
Volume 10 ISBN 0-7734-7703-9
SIL Series 0-88496-738-2

A CIP catalog record for this book is available from the British Library.

The Edwin Mellen Press   The Edwin Mellen Press
Box 450   Box 67
Lewiston, New York   Queenston, Ontario
USA 14092-0450   CANADA L0S 1L0

The Edwin Mellen Press, Ltd.
Lampeter, Ceredigion, Wales
UNITED KINGDOM SA48 8LT

Printed in the United States of America

In Memory of my parents

TABLE OF CONTENTS

FOREWORD

The purpose of this study is to focus on three Italian dramatists, and assess their significance in relation to their times and to each other. In this way I believe that links previously untapped, can be traced, analyzed and demonstrated. The evolution of the dramatic form from the mid-nineteenth century to the early twentieth century may thus be seen in terms of a true literary revolution involving the symbolic presentation of deformity as a prelude to deconstruction and reform. The poet librettist Francesco Maria Piave has seldom been accorded more than a passing comment. His influence on later Italian literature has been ignored. I wish to establish his contribution to the 'duality', regarded the invention of the Milanese Scapigliati and to access the influence of Piave and Boito on the formation of a psychologically oriented literature in which the 'self image' is externalized. I have concentrated on the following works: Piave, *Rigoletto*; Boito, *Libro dei versi – Re Orso, Mefistofele, Otello;* Pirandello, *Il berreto a sonagli*. The validity of my argument may be judged by the reader.

Deirdre O'Grady
November 1999

PREFACE

The notion that spoken drama and sung drama might be studied and related as part of a single cultural continuum has been slow to take root in modern scholarship. Theatre is studied by those who categorize themselves as literary critics or theatre historians, and opera is studied by those who call themselves musicologists - with the separation being certified by the well-kown dictum that in opera 'the composer is the dramatist'. There is truth in that statement which is difficult to refute in itself but its implications for the critic can none the less be exaggerated. Together with the institutional gulf between the two academic disciplines, it inclines scholars to give insufficient weight to the verbal text of an opera, and to the contribution and personality of its librettist. (Lorenzo Da Ponte may be an exception here, but his case is not enough to break the mould.) In particular, there is a tendency to ignore the simple fact that the librettist himself not only belongs to, and is influenced by, the cultural context of his time, but that he in turn can influence and contribute to what comes after him, in the theatre (spoken and sung) and outside it. One of the virtues of this present study by Deirdre O'Grady (who has never shared the above tendency) is that it offers a seamless thesis which gives equal weight to works by figures as diverse as Victor Hugo, Francesco Maria Piave, Arrigo Boito, and Luigi Pirandello, and in pursuing this story she takes in works of lyric and narrative poetry as well as theatre scripts and opera libretti. Not only are the words of operas taken seriously, but they are seen to belong (as logically they must belong) to the mainstream movement of ideas and of artistic forms within their own era.

The era, or eras, addressed by this book cover a century of European cultural history: a period during which. as is common knowledge, large-scale and even revolutionary changes took place in so many fields of human life and thought. Since the seminal study of Mario Praz, we have known something about the Romantic fascination with evil, horror and distortion. which is set alongside an equal preoccupation with absolute beauty and goodness. Such issues rapidly became a central part of what might otherwise have been a purely aesthetic revolution against the principles of Classical art, which at that time were felt to have ruin their course. Deirdre O'Grady pursues these themes and confrontations as a form of 'dualism', tracing their appearance and their continuous development through the works of writers not previously much associated with one another. She also makes clear how these ideas could involve yet another dualistic confrontation: one between large-scale absolute and abstract concepts of traditional morality and traditional art, and the (sometimes literally) 'dissecting' analytic mindset obsessed with the concrete, which was then associated with the rise of modern science.

At the centre of all these conflicts - good *versus* evil, old art *versus* new art, abstract *versus* concrete, synthesis *versus* analysis - stands the concept of a unitary human personality or identity. The notorious challenges thrown up against that concept by Luigi Pirauddlo, at the beginning of the twentieth century, are seen to have a much longer history than is often recognized. It is a salutary experience for an Italianist to see the perhaps over-researched Pirandello related back to the under-researched bohemian moment of the Scapigliatura Milanese. The cap and bells of *Il berretto a sonagli* is traced back to Hugo's jester Triboulet in *Le Roi s'a-muse*, nearly a hundred years before - and we see that this is not simply a matter of the re-use of an external image, but two aspects of a long-developing inquiry into the fragmentary nature of the single human being.

Since we are speaking of jesters, we can add in conclusion that this study offers food for thought for anyone concerned with the uses made of comedy and laugh-ter in successive human societies. Deirdre O'Grady fuels here a number of notions about the reluctance of the Romantic period to take 'the comic' at its face value. There had been a steadily growing perception, based on sympathy and *sensibilité*, that events which make a spectator or reader laugh are often not funny at all for the participants - once one chooses to treat fictional characters actually as human beings - and thus that comedy can co-exist with, or even be identified with, great pain. This, arguably, made it difficult, in this period, for pure comedy to find itself at the cutting edge of innovative art. But it did, in compensation, raise all kinds of insights about the mingling of laughter and tears in fiction, arid about the tensions which occur between them in human life. Fine distinctions. came to be made between different modes of 'comedy', or of what some then preferred to call 'humour'. In Italian, the necessity of creating the word *umorismo* can bring us back to Pirandello once again.

Richard Andrews
University of Leeds

ACKNOWLEDGEMENTS

I here wish to thank most sincerely all who have made this publication possible. I will begin by expressing my gratitude to the staff of the following Libraries and Institutions who came to my aid: the Biblioteca Marciana, Venice, the University of Venice at Ca' Nani Mocenigo, the Fondazione Giorgio Cini, Venice (with special thanks to Maria Teresa Muraro), and the staff of the Main Library, University College Dublin, who were a constant source of information.

I would also like to thank Professor Irene Mamzcarz of the Institute of Scientific Research, Paris, who has helped cultivate my enthusiasm for all aspects of the dramatic form. Gratitude is also due to my head of department, Professor John C. Barnes, University College Dublin, who facilitated my research by organizing 'block teaching' in the academic session 1998-99, thus allowing me free periods for research and writing. I pay tribute also to my typist and type setter, Anne Spillane for her trojan dedication and tolerance in the final stages of the work. My artist Jennifer Petrie, in her cover design, has visually portrayed my three principal poetic symbols: Jester, Demon and Puppet. To her much thanks is due.

Without the good-will of Professor Richard Andrews, Professor of Italian, University of Leeds, Professor Susan Bassnett, Professor of British and Comparative Cultural Studies, University of Warwick, and the scholar and drama critic Dr Joe Farrell, Head of The Italian Department, University of Strathclyde, this book could never have come to print.

Finally I must state by depth of gratitude to my students, whose lively contributions in tutorial discussions, aided the development and association of ideas.

To all,   **Deirdre O'Grady**
Mille Grazie.   **University College Dublin**

INTRODUCTION

The present work traces and evaluates the development and innovation presented in dramatic forms from the post-Romantic to the early Modernist period, by means of a study and analysis of three outstanding contributors: Francesco Maria Piave (1810-76), Arrigo Boito (1842-1918) and Luigi Pirandello (1867-1936). I first considered the topic while researching sources of Pirandello's comedies projecting psychological states, and in particular *Il berretto a sonagli* (*The Cap with Bells*–1820). This work evolves in terms of a series of opposites: possibility/probability, suspicions/facts, doubt/certainty and truth/falsehood. The male protagonist Ciampa vies with the female lead Beatrice to control events, and direct and manipulate the development of a situation. The work projects the human psyche as a clock, functioning through the alternate use of three strings: the serious, the civil and the mad. At the conclusion the successful contender for dominance reduces his rival to the level of puppet, to be manipulated by the puppet master. As the 'mad' string is pulled, madness is juxtaposed with reason, but also emerges as a *rational* solution. In a society dominated by social and moral conventions, truth as an expression of freedom may only be uttered in madness. Beatrice is forced to wear the Jester's cap, originally employed by a *male* jester, with a licence to overturn society.

As a result of cynicism, calculation, and rationalisation, bordering on the unhealthy, spontaneity, emotion and sexual jealousy (expressed by Beatrice) lead to the deprivation of physical freedom. Ironically this loss of freedom allows for the free expression of opinion, labelled 'madness' by a self-righteous society. Although Pirandello witnessed mental illness at close quarters, as a result of the psychological disturbance of his wife, nonetheless, themes and sources of his ideas, I believe, exist in the Italian literature of the post-Romantic and early Modernist period. This book looks to the poetry of the *Scapigliatura Milanese* and the librettos of Arrigo Boito and Francesco Maria Piave. It stresses the influence of *drama* on *drama for music*, and of the latter on the progression from the theatre of the grotesque to that of the absurd.

The concept of manipulation and possession of the conscience and consciousness of the individual can be tapped with reference to Boito's adaptation of Shakespeare's *Othello* (1887) for Giuseppe Verdi. One witnesses a shifting in emphasis from the Elizabethan juxtaposition of Machiavellian prowess and unsophisticated honesty, to the exposition of the entire psyche, as uncertainty and doubt bring about a physical and psychological collapse. The white devil, diabolical reason, takes possession of the mind and thoughts of a black angel. It echoes the latter's words in order to ponder, pervert and reinvent. While Pirandello *externalises* and *reduces* the process in scale, by grotesquely identifying the participants with puppets, Boito provides an internal struggle of gigantic proportions, with Othello rising to a heroic level. The conflict between Art & Science, expressed throughout Boito's *Libro dei versi*, ranges from the scientific application of poetic form ('Dualismo') and the preservation of Art by scientific means ('A una mummia', 'Un torso') to the destruction of poetry by scientific critical analysis ('Lezione d'anatomia'). It is *dramatically* personified in *Otello*. In the poem 'Lezione d'anatomia' the young girl: *era giovane, era bionda, era bella* (*she was young, she was fairhaired, she was beautiful*) is not only the passive figure, dissected and laid bare in the pursuit of forensic science. She is poetry – the work of art analysed, dissected and grotesquely reconstructed to serve the interests of literary criticism. While Boito, towards the end of the nineteenth century would appear to utilize the 'persona' in order to proceed to a *theoretic* assessment of being and behaviour, Pirandello in *Il berretto a sonagli* takes his point of departure from *abstract* ideas, illustrated through *dramatic personification* and reduced not to tragic events, but to comical ones. Psychological realism for Pirandello, is the destruction of the unity of the human *persona*, which is replaced by a mere puppet, the symbol of self gratification and social hypocrisy.

Pirandello, in *Il berretto a sonagli* displaces the relationship between Servants and Masters and replaces the laughter of happiness with that of insanity. A line in Piave's *Rigoletto* (1851), adapted from Victor Hugo's *Le roi s'amuse* (1832), closely resembles Ciampa's assessment of his relationship to his social superior. Piave, as Boito and Pirandello, provide opposites such as light/darkness, laughter/tears, beauty/ugliness. In *Rigoletto* they emanate from an ugly Jester, possessed by the fear of the psychological implications of a curse.

Working forward then, from *Rigoletto*, we proceed from a grotesque, hunchback Jester, to the highly intellectualized process at work in *Otello*, to arrive at a situation in which a *female* wears the Jester's cap of *feigned* and licensed madness, in order to illustrate the absurdity of early twentieth-century Sicilian society.

This study assesses the significance of the dramatic implementation of themes ranging from romantic love, betrayal and self sacrifice to psychological manipulation of behaviour and the juxtaposition of the conscious and subconscious identifiable with twentieth-century Modernism. Fundamental to the entire discussion is the theoretic consideration of *form* and the need for *reform*, by means of deconstruction of poetics and the revitalization of Art by identifying poetry and musical expression. The physical deformity of *Le roi s'amuse* and *Rigoletto* yields to artistic deformity in 'Un torso' and *Re Orso*. The various stages of psychological collapse are witnessed in *Otello*, while mental deformity is cultivated and ridiculed in *Il berretto a sonagli*.

CHAPTER I

The Jester's Revenge

By the middle of the nineteenth century, the original impetus and originality of the romantic movement had given way to a more objective assessment of the times throughout Europe. As early as the 1830's, in France Stendhal had employed realistic symbolism in *Le rouge et le noir* (*The Black and the White*) (1831) and *La Chartreuse de Parma* (*The Charterhouse of Parma*) (1839). Honoré de Balzac (1799-1850), in his novels, reproduced the everyday, humdrum existence of the masses, providing the characterization of unlikeable types, and illustrating the influence of environment on behaviour. As interest in the sciences developed, the study of behavioural science was initiated through the projection of character development, or its disintegration, depending on the fortune or misfortune of the individual within his or her social strata. *Le Père Goriot* (1834) and *Cousine Bette* (1847) both reflect personal deprivation and its effect on relationships. Emile Zola in *Thérèse Raquin* (1867), *L'assomoir* (*The Tavern*) (1877) and *Nana* (1880) brought to life the world of the courtesan and the back-street tavern as he both shocked and moved his readers. The result of the appearance of these narrative works was a growing readership demanding easily read material depicting tragedy and deprivation as it was, rather than as previously presented by romantic visionaries. Realism allied to scientific and sociological pursuits paved the way for social revolt, without, however, in France, totally discarding its romantic origins.

Italian realism reached its high point in depicting provincialism, peasant existence and the lives of miners, fisher folk and olive pickers, complete with local colour. The outstanding writers, who represented a new code of storytelling were Luigi Capuana[1] and Giovanni Verga[2] (1840-1922). Verga, as a preface to his short story 'L'amante di Gramigna' in the collection *Vita dei campi* (*Life in the Fields*) (1880), provides a letter to his friend and colleague Salvatore Farina, in which he explains and illustrates his literary technique.[3] Breaking events down to their most basic, he provides points of departure and arrival in logical and objective terms. The characters speak the language of their primitive world, wear the dress of their folk tradition and demonstrate their attitudes through movement and gesture. In the projection of a situation reduced to its bare essentials, the hand of the writer remains invisible. The story would appear to have written itself.

The subsequent popularity of Verga, and his immediate appeal to those striving for social renewal based on economic principles lead to his definition and acceptance as the father of Italian realism. His desire in later years to provide a more complete social vision than that depicted in the selections of short stories *Vita dei Campi* (1880) and *Novelle rusticane* (*Rustic Short-Stories*) (1883), lead to a projected series of novels, in the style of Balzac's *Human Comedy*. Verga managed only to complete one work: *Mastro-don Gesualdo* (1889), the story of a master builder who constructs his house and his destiny with his own hands. Striving for social advancement, he marries into the local impoverished nobility, and provides it with the financial security it lacked. The protagonist however, rather than build a bridge between the classes, creates complete alienation, as he finds himself rejected by both aristocratic and peasant societies. The intended sequels were to be *La Duchessa di Lyra* (*The Duchess of Lyra*), *L'Onorevole Scipione* (*Deputy Scipione*) and *L'uomo di lusso* (*The Man of Luxury*). These planned novels sought to carry the realistic vision and technique through the Lyra Palace at Palermo, the Quirinale in Rome, and the boardrooms of Milan. The keynote was finance, as deprivation yielded to affluence in the pursuit of economic pathos, realistically perceived.

Critical acclaim and literary historians have conferred the title of *Caposcuola* of realism on Giovanni Verga, yet he is rarely associated with the development of Modernism. His technique provided a lens through which observation replaced contact, and objective assessment of character and situation ruled out any close associations on the part of the reader. The psychological process is demonstrated in terms of character reaction: it is externalized. We witness no internal struggle, nor are we given any material which can be held up for psychological analysis. In other words, Verga has created a unique world, a law unto itself. He has founded a literary movement of which he is the sole exponent.

Romantic Realism did however emerge and thrive in Italy, and its progress can be clearly traced in dramatic form. Its study, however, brings together drama and *melodrama* or opera. A comparative approach to themes, and symbolic figures such

2

as Jesters and Puppets, which carry the tone from the sublime to the ridiculous, from tragedy to comedy, from grotesque to absurd, can throw new light on the development of literary genres during the late nineteenth and early twentieth century. The missing link in previous studies tracing the evolution of Romantic Realism to Modernism is the operatic text: the libretto, often the work of a gifted poet, competent critic or dramatist. Rather than studied as a genre apart, the libretto must be assessed in relation to the literary climate of its day, at times original, often derivative, it can never be ignored. It is central to any consideration of nineteenth-century dramatic form, and, as I wish to demonstrate, is also central to the evolution of early Modernist literature. It is for this reason that Francesco Maria Piave's *Rigoletto* is not merely a good text, but within the Italian context, a highly original one, fusing genres, in a novel approach to the conflict between servants and masters, where the former manipulates, but destiny smiles on the latter: where might is right and Good must perish in the presence of Evil. An assessment of its source, Victor Hugo's *Le roi s'amuse*,[4] and an analysis of Piave's text as the herald to the *Dualismo* or 'Dualism' of the Scapigliatura Milanese (the Milanese bohemian movement of the second half of the century) demonstrates the significance of Hugo's work in the field of *melodrama* or Italian Opera and its influence on Italian thought.

Giuseppe Verdi's early operatic compositions were devoted to historical and political drama.[5] In bringing to life biblical figures and medieval religious conflicts he made a significant contribution to growing Italian patriotic feeling during the struggle for independence.[6] By 1850 however, with the period of the Risorgimento over, Verdi's creative genius was being employed in a new direction. Following the example of the French novelists and dramatists of the period, the operatic theatre moved towards a more intimate and psychologically oriented projection of character, in a world tainted by hypocrisy and ambiguity. When Verdi was invited to write a new opera for the Fenice theatre in Venice in early 1850, he contacted his librettist Francesco Maria Piave,[7] with whom he had successfully collaborated on *Ernani* (1844), *I due Foscari* (1844) and *Stiffelio* (1850). Eventually they settled on Victor Hugo, *Le roi s'amuse*, which had been produced in Paris, at the Théâtre Francais, on 22 November 1832. The subject is the manipulation of the corrupt King, Francis I of France, by his hunchback Jester Triboulet. It also highlights the rôle played by the Jester in the abduction of the wives of courtiers for the King's amusement. When Triboulet is cursed by M. de Saint-Vallier, on account of the dishonouring of Diane de Poitiers, the drama becomes one of psychological conflict between the forces of light and darkness. The political dimension is central to Hugo's work. In demonstrating the corruption of the French Renaissance Court, Hugo wished to issue an invective against absolute power.[8] Verdi and Piave decided to avoid the political issue and introduce the tragedy of a father, in keeping with the theme of family relationships with which he was preoccupied at this time.[9] In focusing on his protagonist he highlighted the rôle of the Jester, walking a tightrope between reality and jest, assuming a manipulative role at Court. In addition, the symbolism of brute ugliness and deformity served to carry the drama a step further towards realism and the grotesque.

Hugo's Jester Triboulet can be historically identified.[10] He was a Court Fool, in the service of Francis I of France. His exploits were celebrated in poetry, drama, vaudeville and historical documentation. Jesters or licensed fools existed in the early history of almost all cultures.[11] At the time of the fall of the Roman Empire, cripples and hunchbacks were often taken under the protection of a master who they might entertain. Nask-ed-Din, the Turkish Jester of Tamerlane in the fourteenth century, became a legend in his lifetime. During the Italian Renaissance, hunchback Court Jesters made their living by steering a precarious course between wit and malice, flattery and insult. In England, the Fool or Clown developed from the figure of vice, the personification of evil in the medieval morality plays. In the Elizabethan theatre he assumes the role of philosopher and exponent of human misery. In Shakespeare's *King Lear* he is depicted as a wise man. Feste, the Fool in *Twelfth Night*, emerges as a philosopher, providing a signpost to action and interaction, and commentary on the events on stage. Lancelot Gobbo, the Clown of *The Merchant of Venice* is clearly a hunchback,[12] while Gratiano's cry 'Let me play the fool!' provides an association with Harlequin, the astute and often sad servant of the *Commedia dell'Arte*.[13]

The Jester's costume had much in common with the Harlequin dress of multicoloured patches, reflecting the poverty of the servant. This was introduced into France from Italy in the sixteenth century by Commedia dell'Arte actors. The hunchback's misery was reflected in his ridiculous attire, containing bizarre and disproportionate elements. If at Court the King represented the sublime, his Jester stood for the ridiculous. He emerged as a parody on the King: in place of a crown he wore a cap with bells, often decorated with a feather, a cockscomb or ass's ears. The feather and cockscomb call to mind the frequent association of fools and madmen with birds. The tinkling of the bells were apt to deafen its wearer to events out-side his cap. The cap later became symbolic of madness and as such is utilized by Luigi Pirandello in *Il berretto a sonagli*. In place of the King's sceptre, the Jester carried a bauble, capped with an emblematic replica of his own head. It stood for his verbal power at Court. With it he carried out a variety of tricks ranging from the clever to the obscene. It served as a confidant, with whom he could carry out conversations. It was to a certain extent his puppet, a forerunner to the ventrilo-quist's doll. The cloak worn by the Jester, was a reminder of his regal state. It was trimmed, not with ermine and gold, but with pompoms, for comic effect. A clear connection may be established between the frolicking and jests played out at the medieval carnival and later adopted by the Commedia dell'Arte troupes of actors, and the antics of the Court Jester. The latter, as clever servant, often outwitted his master and his licensed use of language overturned social convention for the pur-pose of amusement. Victor Hugo's drama depicting the pathetic and malevolent Triboulet explored new areas of the human psyche. It carried the figure of the Clown/Fool to a new level of misery. Paradoxically, this Jester does not amuse. The grotesque nature of the subject matter of the work and its protagonist does not lead to parody but to grotesque tragedy. Triboulet as Jester and father, transcends the role of mere entertainer, and occupies a position between man and brute.

The original Triboulet was called Feurial. He was born at Foiz-les-Blois in France in 1479, and died around 1536.[14] Severely deformed, he was taken under the protection of Louis XII and appointed King's Fool. On the death of Louis he served his successor Francis I. His portrait by Bonifazio hangs in the Louvre. Bonaventure des Périers[15] describes him as a poor idiot. One of the secrets of his success as a Jester lay in his good nature and innocent jests. It is surprising then, that Hugo will transform the good natured innocence to malice. It may well repre-sent an example of his confrontation of Good and Evil. Jean Marot, a contempo-rary of the Jester, spoke of him as having: Little forehead, great eyes, a big nose, figure bent, long flat stomach – a hunched back. Rabelais, another contemporary, in his Panurge wrote that in place of Fool's Day, one ought to celebrate Triboulet day. He called him a good natured honest Fool.[16]

Hugo's interest in the figure of the Jester and its dramatic potential may be traced to a letter written to Alfred de Vigny of 21 April, 1821.[17] In this he acknowl-edges the existence of Emile Deschamps *Fou du Roi*. He may also have been influ-enced by his friend Paul Lecroix's novel *Les deux fous* (*The Two Fools*) (1830). It describes a confrontation between King and Fool, with the destruction of the latter. In Hugo's drama *Cromwell* (1827), there are no less than four Jesters,[18] while Quasimodo, of *Notre Dame de Paris*[19] bears some resemblance to Triboulet. That Hugo is obsessed with the grotesque and deformity there can be little doubt. *L'homme qui rit* is based on the misfortune of one who is forced to laugh permanently for *physical* as opposed to *professional* reasons. The distorted expression, forced into a sinister smile, is the absolute expression of human tragedy, deprived of words. What is obvious is that Hugo, in *Le roi s'amuse* is using a traditionally comic figure, the Jester with attributes of a wise man, and the Italian Harlequin, in order to question absolute rule, rank and the relationship between servant and master. This in itself is not original. A similar topic, centred on the feudal rights of the aristocrat, and the servant's opposition of such rights was treated by Caron de Beaumarchais in his trilogy *Le Barbier de Seville* (*The Barber of Seville*) 1775, *Le Marriage de Figaro* (*The Marriage of Figaro*) 1784 and *La Mère Coupable* (*The Guilty Mother*) 1792. But while Beaumarchais provides an enlightened couple, Figaro and Suzanne, (the comic descendants of Arlecchino/Harlequin and Colombina, who indulge in a sophisticated salon comedy, with revolutionary innuendoes), Hugo provides a bitter battle between light and darkness, laughter and tears, the ugly and the beautiful, and between servant and master, which contains none of the charm of Beaumarchais' comedy.

There was one performance of Victor Hugo's *Le roi s'amuse* in 1832. On the day following the production Hugo received the news that the work was to be suspended. The suspension became a prohibition within twenty four hours. The government of Louis Philippe prohibited the piece, which continued to be banned during the Second Empire, when Hugo himself was in political exile. In 1873, under the Third Republic, it was banned again. When it was finally given a hearing in 1882, fifty years after the initial fiasco, it was greeted by silence, at a time when its adaptation by Francesco Maria Piave for Giuseppe Verdi, had made it one of the most popular pieces in the operatic repertoire. It is Verdi's opera which has saved the drama from complete obscurity. Although dismayed at the news that his play was to become an opera, Hugo is reported to have relented on hearing the music.

On hearing of the suspension of his tragedy *Le roi s'amuse* Hugo attempted to vindicate his freedom of expression by acting through the courts.[20] He defended the moral of his work, insisting that its true subject was the curse placed on Triboulet by St. Vallier. He provides an outline of the plot and a dramatic descrip-

6

tion of the character of Triboulet:

Why is the piece considered immoral? Is it because of the plot? The plot is as follows: Triboulet is deformed, Triboulet is ill, Triboulet is the Court Jester... Triboulet hates the King because he is the King, the gentry because they are the gentry, ordinary men because they are not hunchbacks.....He corrupts the King, and pushes him towards tyranny and vice. In Triboulet's hands the King is nothing more than a puppet..... M. de Saint Vallier forces his way into the King's presence and rebukes him on account of the dishonouring of Diane de Poitiers. Triboulet insults him, and M. de Saint Vallier raises his arms and curses Triboulet. ...The true subject of the drama is the curse of M. de Saint Vallier. On whom does this curse fall? On Triboulet, the King's clown? No, on Triboulet the man, who has a heart, who has a daughter. The same King whom Triboulet encourages to indulge in fornication, seduces Triboulet's daughter. The clown is struck by destiny in the same manner as M. de Saint Vallier.the curse of Diane's father is effected on Blanche's father.[21]

Two important aspects of the plot emerge from Hugo's condensation of it: the fundamental importance of the curse, and the manipulative qualities of Triboulet. He attempts to assume the role of puppet master, in an attempt to control events, only to be defeated by supernatural forces, with implications of the macabre and the sub-conscious. The juxtaposition of laughter and tears underlining the fusion of the comic and the tragic genres through the *persona* of the Jester demonstrates Hugo's dramatic updating and remoulding of the clown of the Italian comic theatre. No longer wearing the Jester costume (Triboulet is enveloped in his cloak) Hugo in the two great monologues, Act II.2 and Act V.1, has demasked the clown and provided in its place a man demented, tormented to the point of turning his verbal pungency to physical violence:

Triboulet: Ah! la nature et les hommes m'ont fait
               Bien méchant, bien cruel et bien lâche en effet.
               O rage! être bouffon! O rage être difforme
               Toujours cette pensée! et qu'on veille ou qu'on dorme,
               Quand du monde en rêvant vous avez fait le tour
               Retomber sur ceci: Je suis bouffon de cour!
               Ne vouloir ne pouvoir, ne devoir et ne faire
               Que rire![22]

(Ah! nature and mankind have in fact made me Truly malicious,
cruel and cowardly.
Oh what anger! to be a Jester. Oh what anger
To be deformed. Always this thought, awake and asleep.
And when you have crossed the whole world in a dream
To fall back on this: I am the Court Jester unable to wish,
or to be able, or to have to do other than laugh.)

He contrasts his image with that of his master:

Triboulet: Grand, jeune, et bien portant, et roi de France, et beau,
                      Me pousse avec le pied dans l'ombre où je
                      soupire,
                      Et me dit en baillant: Bouffon! Fais-moi
                      donc rire!
                      O pauvre fou de cour! – C'est un homme, après tout.[23]

(Great, young and well built, handsome, the King of France.
He taps me with his foot, in the shade where I doze
And he says to me sleepily: Now Jester, make me laugh!
Oh unfortunate Court Fool! He is a man, after all.)

Laughter is identified with malice, inferiority and despair. The Jester in meeting the
King's command, must make him laugh, must turn reality on its head. Triboulet,
however, determines the parody of the grotesque by reducing the King to an
essence inferior to the Jester i.e. the puppet. With the manipulation of order and
events the lower essence must conquer the higher i.e. the Jester the King: the Jester
the Puppet. In so doing Triboulet aspires towards the introduction of a new laughter, devoid of masks:

Triboulet: Je vais donc me venger! – Enfín! la chose est faite –
                      Voici bientôt un mois que j'attends, que je guette,
                      Resté bouffon, cachant mon trouble intérieur,
                      Pleurant des pleurs de sang sous mon masque
                      rieur.[24]

(I am about to avenge myself! At last!
The thing is done –
Soon it will be a month that I wait, watch
Staying Jester hiding my inner torment,
Weeping tears of blood behind my laughing mask.)

As Triboulet waits to receive the body of the King, the elements contribute to the creation of an atmosphere in which the supernatural forces will dominate. The cry of the Jester is the final verbal attempt, on the part of the grotesque to conquer:

Triboulet: Oh! jouis, vil bouffon, dans ta fierté profond.
                La vengeance d'un fou fait osciller le monde.[25]

                (Rejoice, wretched Jester in your deep pride
                The vengeance of a fool makes the world tremble.)

The battle between Triboulet and destiny is realistically conceived by Hugo in such a way that dramatically the action appears a conflict between the writer and his tragic hero. The 'coup de grace' is effected with the parody of the grotesque, providing shock effect combined with pathos:

Triboulet: J'ai tué mon enfant! J'ai tué mon enfant.[26]

                (I have killed my child! I have killed my child.)

Triboulet is finally established as a man, a father and tragic hero without recourse to feigned laughter but to natural tears.

Giuseppe Verdi instantly recognized the potential of the dramatic 'tour de force' contained in *Le roi s'amuse*. In a letter to Francesco Maria Piave he states: "Oh *Le roi s'amuse* è il più gran soggetto e forse il più gran dramma dei tempi moderni. Triboulet è creazione degna di Shakespeare".[27] (*Le roi s'amuse* is the greatest subject and perhaps the greatest drama of modern times. Triboulet is a creation worthy of Shakespeare). After many censorship difficulties,[28] Piave's drama finally reached the stage. The dramatic situations in Hugo's play were unaltered. The settings and the names of the characters were changed.[29] The action was transferred to Mantua and Francis I became a Duke, Triboulet became Rigoletto, deriving from 'rigoler', the French word for 'guffaw', and Blanche became Gilda. That was not the end of the story, however. In order to pass the censors in various Italian provinces it was performed under a variety of titles including *Lionello*, *Clara di Perth* and *Viscardello*.

Hugo's influence on the Italian operatic libretto is considerable. However, his significance as one who prompted imitation in the poetic and dramatic field has, however, never been explored. Piave's adaptation of *Le roi s'amuse* for the operatic stage is not our main concern in this study. What is of foremost importance is that Hugo transformed the stereotype into a tragic hero. As Carlo Goldoni unmasked the much loved yet predictable caricatures of the eighteenth-century Commedia dell'Arte,[30] Hugo dramatically demonstrated the humanity of the clown. In providing complexity of character he juxtaposed and identified laughter and tears, light and shade, good and evil while decrying political and social absolutism. It may be said that Piave condensed the text, taking what aspects best converted to the dramatic form, and to the musical demands of the composer. He carried the antithesis further than his source, making use of contrasting images in the stage description and stage direction. He provided *two diverse* poetic forms: the Arcadian poetic grace and elegance of the traditional libretto, which accompany the adventures of the Duke of Mantua. A totally original and psychologically oriented dramatic declaration became the language of Rigoletto the Jester. The contrast was further highlighted by the composer who cast the Duke as a lyric tenor and Rigoletto as a dramatic baritone. Gilda's musical role is that of a lyric coloratura soprano, Maddalena's darker tones are those of a mezzo contralto. The psychological drama which Piave created was further accentuated by Verdi's early intention of calling the work *La Maledizione* (*The Curse*). In place of Hugo's pathetic 'J'ai tué mon enfant' (I have killed my child), Piave's drama concludes with Rigoletto's demented cry: 'Ah! la maledizione' (Ah! the curse). The transformation of *Le roi s'amuse* marks the entry into Italian literature of a fusion of genres, of dramatic antithesis and a discourse on evil, all of which prepare the way for the 'Dualism' of the *Scapigliatura Milanese* and the poetry and drama of Arrigo Boito.

The co-existence of Good and Evil in Rigoletto is not merely contained in the characters, or communicated through words and actions, but it is integrated into the structure of the drama by Piave. The opera is in three acts. The first act is divided into two scenes: an interior and an exterior. The first scene represents: 'una sala magnifica...splendidamente illuminata...gran costume, festa nel suo pieno.[31] (A magnificent Hall...brilliantly illuminated...rich attire, the celebrations at their height). The second scene, in contrast shows: 'l'estremità di una via cieca, a sinistra una casa di discreta apparenza con una piccola corte circondata da muro. A destra della via è il muro altissimo del giardino e in fianco del palazzo di Ceprano. È notte.[32] (The end of a cul-de-sac, left a house of fairly good appearance with a small courtyard enclosed by a wall...To the right of the road a very high garden wall and one side of the Ceprano Palace. It is night.)

The second act contains one scene: in the libretto the description is as follows: 'Vi sono due porte laterali una maggiore in fondo che si chiude. Ai suoi lati pendono i ritratti, in tutta figura, a sinistra del Duca, a destra della sua sposa.'[33] (There is a door on each side, and a larger one at the far end, flanked by full length portraits. On the left, there is one of the Duke, on the right, one of his wife.) The final act contains just one scene. It is divided in two, as the second scene of the first act: 'É la sponda destra del Mincio. A sinistra è una casa a due piani...nella facciata che guarda la strada è una porta che si apre per di dentro. ...al di là del fiume è Mantova'.[34] (It is the right bank of the river Mincio. To the left a two storey house. On the wall facing the street there is a door which goes inwards. ...beyond the river is Mantua).

The symbolic function of left and right is apparent from the commencement of the drama, as is the 'double awareness' of the spectator with regard to actions within and without in Act I.2 and Act III.2. In Act II, Rigoletto, already assuming the rôle of betrayed father enters, from the right hand side. Gilda, at the conclusion of the work, runs to her death from right to left. The river Mincio also contributes to the symbolism of direction: it, as the Adda in Manzoni's novel *I promessi sposi* separates freedom from chaos. Rigoletto and Gilda have already crossed the boundary and are facing in the direction of Verona. Paradoxically to the left of the right bank is the tavern with the prostitute Maddalena and the Duke of Mantua. The outdoor settings are enveloped in darkness. The entire action takes place at night. The interior scenes are magnificently illuminated with artificial lighting, also symbolic of the corruption of the Ducal Court.

The symbolism of place and movement is continued, when one considers that

11

Piave has provided two heroes: the romantic and the realistic. It could be argued that the latter is cast as an anti-hero. However by the conclusion of the piece Rigoletto has been redeemed in the eyes of the public and assumes the role of the tragic hero par excellence. Linguistically the Duke of Mantua is identifiable with the refined elegance of the eighteenth-century libretto, modelled on the Arcadian poetic form.[35] His first aria, communicating immoral libertinism and the ethic of the Renaissance pastoral world: *se piace ei lice*,[36] contains the personification of abstractions, particular to the seventeenth and eighteenth century 'aria antica':

Duca: La costanza tiranna del core

                    Detestiamo qual morbo crudele.

                    Sol chi vuole si serbi fedele:

                    No v'ha amor se non v'è libertà.[37]

                                  Rigoletto Act I.1.

                    (Fidelity the tyrant of the heart

                    We detest like a pestilence

                    Only he who wishes so, should remain faithful

                    Without freedom, there is no love.)

In the final scene of the opera, the Duke's other famous set-piece 'La donna è mobile' (Woman is fickle) is, as the above quoted aria, a light-hearted tune, written in the style of a popular song. It does however contain in its idealogical expression, the entire reversal of the significance of the events hitherto dramatically played out: it is the fidelity of women and the fickleness of men, that carry the action to its tragic conclusion. Herein is introduced the basic confrontation of words and circumstances, which will later be adapted by the writers of Scapigliatura, and by Boito in particular.

Duca: La donna è mobile

                    Qual piuma al vento,

                    muta d'accento

                    e di pensier.

                    Sempre un amabile

                    leggiadro viso

in pianto o in riso

è menzognero.[38]

Rigoletto Act III.2

(Woman is as fickle as a feather in the wind,

with few words and little mind.

Always a lovable, pretty face,

Be it in laughter or tears

it lies.)

In these arias Piave has succeeded in combining the concepts of Renaissance amorality and romantic freedom. However at the level of plot, a realistic force is present: the *actual* cause of the tragedy is the disobedience of Gilda: she allows the Duke enter her home disguised as Gualtier Maldé, against the advice of her father (Act I, 12); she returns to the tavern in order to die for her lover, rather than obey her father's instructions to leave at once for Verona (Act III, 3). By fusing at this point three, rather than two elements: the Renaissance, the Romantic and the Realistic, Piave points to the role of destiny in the plot, and to the ultimate significance of the curse.

The psychological drama surrounding the character of the protagonist is set into motion on his hearing Monterone's curse:

Rigoletto: (Che sento! Orrore!)[39]

Rigoletto Act I, 6.

Rigoletto: (What do I hear! Oh horror!)

It is clear that Rigoletto believes in supernatural forces and that he fears them. The result being, he is psychologically tortured by the recurring thought of the curse. This transforms Rigoletto from an active participant in court life, to a contemplative manipulator in pursuit of revenge: revenge for his deformity, for his condemnation to wear the mask of Jester and ultimately for his daughter's abduction. Circumstances and events combine to create a tragic monster which takes its place as one of the greatest projections of the Italian theatre.[40] Piave has intellectualized his presentation of Rigoletto from his entry, by providing the following words:

Rigoletto: In testa che avete
                  Signor di Ceprano?[41]

                              Rigoletto Act I, 3.

Rigoletto: (What have you on your head
                  Signor Ceprano?)

The introduction of the term 'head' and the ambiguity of its interpretation, as in
Rigoletto's opening address, identifies the image and its symbolic significance.
Rigoletto is carrying the bauble bearing the effigy of his own head, in order to poke
fun at the members of court. The veiled reference to what may be on Ceprano's
head, is obviously interpreted by the Court as an insinuation that he is wearing the
horns of a cuckold. Yet it can also question what may be on his mind as the references to the head are repeated:

Rigoletto: Allora la testa
Duca: Che di, questa testa?
Rigoletto: É ben naturale
                  Che fai di tal testa.[42]

                              Rigoletto Act I, 5.

Rigoletto: (Well then, this head.
Duke: What are you saying, this head?
Rigoletto: Naturally
                  What else is such a head good for?)

It becomes clear that the work is developing as a drama of the mind. As he is lead
away in disgrace to be beheaded, Monterone swears revenge as he promises to
appear as a ghost carrying his skull:

Monterone: Spettro terribile mi rivedrete
                  Portante in mano il teschio mio
                  Vendetta chiedere al mondo e a Dio.[43]

                              Rigoletto Act I, 6.

                  (You shall see me again

14

As a terrifying spectre
Carrying my skull
Asking revenge of God and the world.)

The drama of the mind unfolds as Rigoletto makes his way towards his home, where he is transformed to another man 'in altr'uom qui mi cangio.' No longer wearing the Jester's costume, and enveloped in his cloak, he reviews his fears and his situation in the wake of Monterone's curse. The dramatic monologue occurs as Rigoletto is about to greet Gilda, having spoken with Sparafucile.[44] The monologue 'Pari siamo' (We are equal) presents an important innovation in both the history of drama and of the musical form. Verdi uses declamative recitative in place of the tuneful aria to which we are accustomed. It follows the shifting thoughts within the mind of the character as he once again allows himself be overtaken by fear, in the wake of the curse. The scene is a masterpiece of self-analysis: Rigoletto contrasts his lot with that of the hired assassin: they are equal. He wounds with his tongue, Sparafucile with his dagger. He laughs, the other eliminates. He gives dramatic outlet to his state. He blames man and nature for the ugliness of his body and of his soul:

Rigoletto: O uomini! o natura!...
               Vil scellerato mi faceste voi!...
               O rabbia esser difforme..Esser buffone.
               Non dover, non poter altro che ridere...!
               Il retaggio d'ogni uom m'è tolto...il pianto.[45]
                              Rigoletto Act I, 8.

               (O men! O nature!
               You have made me evil and corrupt.
               What anger, to be deformed...to be a Jester,
               To be permitted nothing but to laugh
               I am denied the human right to weep.)

There follows a further demonstration of Rigoletto's hatred of the courtiers. His role, in making the Duke laugh and finding no outlet for his own rage, is his real torment. In order to take his revenge on nature for its cruelty, he will make the tears of others *his* amusement. Yet later that night when the courtiers decide to abduct the Jester's mistress, the court will laugh at *his* tears. The youth, good looks and position of his master, excite his jealousy:

Rigoletto: Questo padrone mio,
                 Giovin, giocondo, si possente, bello
                 Sonnecchiando mi dice:
                     Fa' ch'io rida buffone![46]
                             Rigoletto Act I, 8.

                 (This master of mime
                 Young, merry, so very powerful, handsome.
                 Half-dozing, says to me
                 Jester, make me laugh!)

At this point in the drama, the conventional conflict between servants and masters, carries the piece, in some respects, close to the world of the Commedia dell'Arte, where the servant wears a costume and a mask, which separates him from refined society, in which conventional attire is worn. Towards the end of the monologue the thought of the curse once again raises its head – Rigoletto is unsure as to why it affects him so.

Rigoletto: Quel vecchio maledivami. Tal pensiero
                 perchè conturba ognor la mente mia?
                 mi coglierà sventura? Ah, no, è follia.[47]
                             Rigoletto Act I, 8.

                 (That old man cursed me. Why does that
                 thought still prey on my mind,
                 Will it bring disaster to fall on me?
                 Ah no, this is madness.)

This is the psychological portrait of Rigoletto. For the first time in the Italian theatre a clown has come face to face within himself, as a man, who subjectively, and objectively assesses his existence. The monologue contains the two semantics

16

which will determine the tone of the work: laughter and tears. It points to a tragedy with comic setting, in which the comic becomes the grotesque. As spectators we logically conclude that Rigoletto's fear and sense of guilt arises from his having laughed at Monterone's sorrow:

> E tu serpente.
> Tu che d'un padre ridi al dolore,
> Sii maledetto.[48]
>
> *Rigoletto* Act I, 6.

> (And you serpent,
> You who laughs at a father's sorrow,
> Be cursed.)

From this point of the opera, through to the conclusion, one witnesses Rigoletto's tears and his immense tragedy. The monologue 'Pari siamo' presents Rigoletto as an emotional giant, expounding varying degrees of anger and disquiet. He towers above the other characters in the work. From this point on the reader/spectator/listener totally identifies and sympathizes with the hunchback's tragedy. (It is significant that Piave has succeeded in highlighting the visual, linguistic and melodic aspect of human drama.) Luigi Baldacci,[49] in his assessment of the scene notes that Piave provides a rhyme on only two occasions in the monologue: buffone/dannazione, mente mia/follia. At this poetic level Piave's intention is clear as 'Jester' rhymes with 'damnation' and 'my mind' with 'madness.' Baldacci concludes that not only has Piave provided Verdi with his 'best' libretto (*il più bello*), but also with the most advanced dramatic medium to date. He makes the surprising, yet highly acceptable statement that Verdi's 'real' librettist was not Boito, but Piave.[50] Giovanna Gronda states that the artistic form in *Rigoletto* was pressing closer to the spoken drama than to the operatic medium, and that certain scenes in the work, i.e. the conclusion of Act I could be seen as mime, within the context of dramatic prose.[51]

In combining comic and tragic attributes, and by introducing the visual dimension, by means of gesture, costume and the confrontation of light and darkness, Piave does not merely utilize dramatic *situations* and psychological probings, he also provides a series of 'key words' which progress through the text. The adven-

17

tures of these provide the key to the interpretation of the work. The re-occurence of the words *riso* (laughter), *pianto* (weeping), *lagrime* (tears) confers complexity on the text. The frivolous laughter of the Duke, compliments the ironic sneering of Rigoletto, which is converted to a free expression of sorrow at the loss of his daughter. The scornful laughter of the courtiers is juxtaposed with Maddalena's amusement. The total transformation of Rigoletto between Acts I and II is demonstrated *visually* by means of two contrasting images of the Jester 'at work.' In Act I, 6. as he approaches Monterone and feigns seriousness, the stage direction dictates (Si avanza con *ridicola gravità*) (He comes forward with ridiculous solemnity). In Act II, 3. Rigoletto enters 'canterellando con represso dolore' (humming with suppressed sorrow). "Tra la-la-la-la-la-la-la," is an attempt to perform as a Jester while reacting as a father. The two situations provide an example of Piave's 'duality' as laughter and sorrow are combined to illustrate sarcasm and pretence in Act I and true sorrow barely concealed in Act II. In these two key moments, comedy and tragedy are merged. In the first instance, the tragedy is that of Monterone, in the second, it is Rigoletto's. In both cases the situation is similar: the abduction and dishonour of a daughter.

The presence of sentiment in *Rigoletto* is first introduced with reference to Rigoletto's dead wife:

Rigoletto: Ella sentia quell'angelo

                  Pietà delle mie pene.[52]

                             Rigoletto Act I, 9.

                  (That angel felt pity on account

                  Of my suffering.)

                  Gilda replies sobbing:

                  Quanto dolor!...Che spremere

                  Si amaro pianto può?[53]

                             Rigoletto Act I, 9.

                  (What sorrow! What can have caused

                  Such bitter tears?)

When Rigoletto consoles his daughter, following her abduction, the expression of sorrow is again touched upon:

18

Piangi, fanciulla e scorrere
Fa il pianto sul mio cor.[54]

Rigoletto Act II, 6.

(Weep, child, and let your tears fall

Upon my breast.)

The confrontation of laughter and tears is finally projected in an antithesis which finds its unity in one of the greatest ensembles of nineteenth-century opera: the quartette. In Act III, 3, Gilda and Rigoletto from the right hand side of the stage, witness the Duke make love to Maddalena, Sparafucile's sister. In a stage set divided in two, laughter and tears combine as a commentary on the infidelity of the Duke. Herein there is contained the contrast between practicality or realism and idealism or romanticism. Maddalena dismisses the Duke's declaration of love, with the laughter of experience. Gilda expresses her disillusionment while Rigoletto promises revenge, stating bluntly that weeping can do no good.

Maddalena: Ah! Ah! Rido ben di core
Ché tai baie costan poco;
Quanto valga il vostro gioco,
Mel credete, so apprezzar.
Sono avvezza, bel signore,
Ad un simile scherzar.

Gilda: Ah, così parlar d'amore
A me pur l'infame ho udito!

Rigoletto: Taci, il piangere non vale;[55]

Rigoletto Act III, 3.

Maddalena: (Ha, Ha. I laugh heartily
Such talk costs little!
Believe me. I know exactly
What such a game costs
I am accustomed, fine Sir

To such jokes.)

Gilda: In the same way I heard
                The scoundrel speak of love to me.

Rigoletto: (Quiet, weeping will do no good.)

To quote Folco Portinari, 'the drama in its ambiguity and double face qualities finds its crux in the Quartette.[56] The varying but consistent poetic and dramatic styles come together as the romantic hero, the Duke, has the main melodic line and the sentimental Gilda soars above him in despair. While Maddalena provides a syncopation on Gilda's lyrical leaps, Rigoletto assumes the role of protector and vindicator. His words in the first section of his contribution, are in its rhyme scheme typical of the conventional poetic style of the romantic libretto. In the second section they resemble conversation, containing practical instructions, as he realistically prepares Gilda for another life in Verona.[57]

    The final contrast under consideration is that between Good and Evil, symbolized by beauty and ugliness, daughter and father, who assume qualities approaching the angelical and the diabolical, Gilda is 'questo fiore' (this flower) Act I, 10., 'donna celeste' (heavenly woman) Act I, 12., 'fata od angiol' (fairy or angel) Act I, 14., 'si pura' (so pure) Act II, 3; Rigoletto is referred to as 'anima nera' (dark/evil soul) Act I.5., 'serpente' (serpent) Act I, 6., Throughout the drama his deformity is indicated as the source of his way way of life. If ugliness is evil, then consequently the Jester represents damnation, his daughter salvation. Reference has already been made to the rhyming of '*buffone*' and '*dannazione*'. Gilda, as beauty and goodness is also an advocate for her father.

Gilda: Lassù...in cielo, vicina alla madre...
                In eterno per voi...pregherò.[58]
                              Rigoletto Act III, 10.

                (Up in heaven, close to my mother.
                I will pray for you forever.)

Although Maddalena cannot be regarded as 'good' in the absolute sense, neither can she be regarded as totally evil. There are conflicting reports of her physical attributes: she is called 'bella' (beautiful) by her brother Sparafucile, yet she dismisses the Duke's compliments responding to

Duca: La bella mano candida
                   (Your lovely white hand)
                   with
Maddalena: Son brutta.[59]
                   (I am ugly.)

Rigoletto Act III, 3.

This is yet another example of the contradictory elements contained in the libretto: as a realist, having (in contrast to Gilda) lived an unsheltered life, Maddalena is capable of *physical* self-assessment, and of distinguishing between sex-appeal and beauty. On assessment of the symbolic function of the characters, one may conclude that *Rigoletto* is a dramatization of the closeness of the forces of light and darkness, and the difficulty of defining their limits. Gilda, as an angel, is the child of a devil. This leads to the questions, in defiance of theological dogma, 'can good be the child of evil?' 'Can ugliness give birth to beauty?' Answered in the affirmative, the work can then be seen as a defiance of orthodox teaching and a prelude to the 'Duality' of Arrigo Boito. As Gilda dies, she promises to pray for her father. He, tearing at his hair cries out in despair:

Rigoletto: Ah! la maledizione.[60]
                   (Ah! the curse.)

The final lines of the drama bring together a prayer and an acknowledgement of the strength of the forces of darkness. Good and Evil are in stark contrast, yet they exist in close proximity. Evil *can* father good, which *can* call on the forces of light in an attempt to redeem darkness. In a world where boundaries are unclear, one may conclude that the antitheses of the work form part of an immense whole: a gripping drama containing opposing forces. We are just a short distance from the confession of Verdi's next great librettist and Scapigliato 'par excellence', Arrigo Boito:

21

Son luce ed ombra; angelica
Farfalla o verme immondo.
Sono un caduto cherubo
Dannato a errar sul mondo.
O un demone che sale
affaticando l'ale
Verso un lontano ciel.[61]

A. Boito 'Dualismo', I. 1-7.

(I am light and shade; angelic
butterfly or filthy worm.
I am a fallen angel
Damned to wander on the earth
Or a rising devil
Beating its wings
Toward a distant heaven.)

Viewed from an historical and stylistic viewpoint the deformed Jester is symbolic of a post-Romantic assessment of Art and its form. It points towards a revised concept of literary symmetry and content. With regard to the co-existence of comic and tragic elements and the close relationship between Good and Evil, manifested by means of traditional poetic forms and dramatic recitative, the conventional tragic piece has itself been 'deformed'. The presence of subtle symbolism introduced through the imagery of the head, mind and *decapitation* demonstrates that Hugo in France and Piave in Italy have effected a revolution in theatrical form. The later poetry of Scapigliatura and the Italian libretto will reflect this change. There will follow a total deconstruction and reinvention of poetic expression and subject matter. This shall be discussed in detail in the following chapter on Scapigliatura and the emerging conflict between Art and Science.

NOTES

1   See C.A. Madrignani, *Capuana e il naturalismo*, Laterza, Bari, 1970; M. Musitelli Paladini, *Nascita di una poetica: il verismo*, Palumbo, Palermo, 1974; C.A. Madrignani, *Regionalismo e naturalismo in Toscana e nel Sud: Collodi, Pratesi, Capuana, De Roberto, Serao*, in LIL, VIII/I, 1975, pp. 511-63; T. Iermano (editor). *Positivismo, Naturalismo, Verismo. Questioni teoriche e analisi critiche*, Vecchierelli, Manziana (Roma), 1996.

2   See: V. Spinazzola, *Verismo e positivismo*, Garzanti, Milan, 1977; S. Rossi, *L'età del verismo*, Palumbo, Palermo, 1978; G. Debenedetti, *Verga e il naturalismo*, Garzanti, Milan, 1976; N. Borsellino, *Storia di Verga*, Laterza, Bari, 1992. G. Carnazzi, 'Verga e i veristi', in SLIV, *L'Ottocento*, III, 1997, pp. 2179-292.

3   See: D. Woolf, *The Art of Verga: a Study in Objectivity*, Sydney University Press, Sydney, 1977, pp. 115 6. There it is argued that Verga, rather than project a fully fledged theory, conveys the germ of an idea. See also, D. O'Grady, 'The Vicious Circle' in E. Haywood and C. Ó Cuilleanaín (editors), *Italian Storytellers*, Irish Academic Press, Dublin, 1989, pp. 204-28.

4   See: A. Ubersfeld (editor), *Victor Hugo, Oeuvres Complètes, Théâtre* I, Robert Laffont, Paris, 1985, pp. 829-968. Of particular interest is the preface, pp. 829-36, which contains Hugo's defence of the piece. See also: A. Ubersfeld, *Le Roi et le Bouffon*, Librairie José Corti, Paris, 1974, pp. 95-156, pp. 509-544; J. Cornuz, *Hugo, l'Homme des Misérables*, Favre, Lausanne, 1985, pp. 314-25; G. Robb, Victor Hugo, Picador, London, 1997.

5   See G. Baldini, *Abitare la battaglia*, Garzanti, Milan, 1970; J. Budden, *The Operas of Verdi*, I. Cassell, London, 1973; M. Mila, *L'arte di Verdi*, Einaudi, Turin, 1980.

6   For a consideration of Verdi's early patriotic opera, and his collaboration with Temistocle Solera, see: L. Miragoli, *Il melodramma italiano dell'Ottocento*, Tipografia delle Mantellate, Rome, 1924; A. Cassi-Ramelli, *Libretti e librettisti*, Ceschina, Milan, 1973; M. Mila, *La Giovinezza di Verdi*, ERI Turin, 1974; See also my chapter 'High Priests and Patriots' in D. O'Grady, *The Last Troubadours: Poetic Drama in Italian Opera*, Routledge, London and New York, 1991, pp. 99-127.

7   Francesco Maria Piave (Murano, Venice, 1810-Milan 1876). Originally studied for the priesthood. On leaving the seminary he was employed as a proof-reader at the Antonelli publishing group in Venice. In 1843, Count Alvise Mocenigo commissioned a libretto for the Fenice Theatre, drawn from the text of Cromwell by Victor Hugo. This was substituted by Ernani, from Hugo's Hernani. This marked the beginning of the Verdi/Piave collaboration. There followed *I due Foscari* (1844), *Macbeth* (1847), *Il Corsaro* (1848), *Stiffelio* (1850), *Rigoletto* (1851), *La traviata* (1853), *Simon Boccanegra* (1857) and *La Forza del destino* (1862). In 1859, he was appointed official poet to La Scala, Milan. In 1867 he suffered a stroke, and lived paralysed for a further nine years. Bibliography: A. Santi, 'Per il centenario della nascita di F.M. Piave', *La voce di Murano*, 18 May, 1910; T. Mantovani, 'F.M. Piave', *Musica d'Oggi*, September 1924, L. Baldacci, *La musica in Italiano: Libretti d'opera dell'Ottocento*, Rizzoli, Milan, 1997, pp. 90-205.

8   For the political events preceeding Hugo's composition of *Le roi s'amuse*, see J. Cornuz, Hugo, L'homme des Miserables, op.cit., pp. 315-17.

9   See D. O'Grady *The Last Troubadours* op.cit., pp. 152-72. Here *Rigoletto, Il trovatore* and *La traviata* are discussed as portraits of family relationships i.e. father/daughter, mother/son, father/son.

10 See A. Ubersfeld *Le roi et le bouffon* op.cit., pp. 95-6, 102. For contemporary accounts see: Rabelais, Tiers Livre Ch. XXXVII Pleiade, pp. 461, 464-7. It is believed that Hugo first became acquainted with the figure of Triboulet in *Brantôme, Vie des grands capitaines français* (Connétable de Montmorenay). See also G. Robb, *Victor Hugo*, op.cit. p. 176.

11 For the historical background to fools and jesters, see: P. Lacroix, *Les Deux Fous. Histoire du temps de Francois Ier, Prècédé d'un essai historique inédit sur les fous en litre d'office*, 2 vols. Delloye et Lecou, Paris, 1837; J. Doran, *A History of Court Fools*, London, 1855; E. Welsford,

The Fool: His Social and Literary History, Faber, London 1935; W. Willford, The Fool and his Sceptre, Northwestern University Press, 1969; P.V.A. Williams (editor), The Fool and the Trickster, D.S. Brewer, Rowman and Littlefield, Cambridge 1979; S. Billington, A Social History of the Fool, The Harvester Press, Sussex, St Martins Press, New York, 1984.

12 Note the term 'gobbo' in Italian means 'hunchback'.

13 The speech, in reply to Antonio's 'I hold the world, but as the world, Gratiano/a stage where everyman must play a part/and mine a sad one'. It must also be argued that the Shakespearian comedies Twelfth Night, and The Merchant of Venice, both of which contain Fools bear strong resemblances, as regards character and plot, to the Commedia dell'Arte form.

14 See: A. Canel, Recherches historiques sur les Fous des Rois de France, Paris, 1873, p. 99.

15 See J. Bonaventure des Périers, Les Contes ou les Nouvelles devis de Bonaventure des Périers, 3 Vols. Amsterdam 1735, I, p. 29, III, p. 37.

16 Rabelais, Tiers Livre, Ch. XXXVII, Pléiade, p. 461.

17 See A. Ubersfeld, Le Roi et le Bouffon, op. cit., p. 95, n. 5.

18 See V. Hugo, Oeuvres Complètès, Théâtre I., op.cit., pp. 5-385.

19 See J. Cornuz, Hugo. L'homme des miserables, op. cit., pp. 152-3. It is interesting to note that laughter is equated with misery by G. Leopardi in 'Elogio degli uccelli', Operette Morali (1824). Leopardi states that man originally laughed in drunkeness in an attempt to hide his misery. See: G. Leopardi, Operette Morali: Rizzoli, Milan, 1951, pp. 168-76.

20 Hugo's entire defence is included in A. Ubersfeld, editor, Victor Hugo, Théâtre, I., op.cit., pp. 839-45.

21 See D. O'Grady, The Last Troubadours, op. cit., pp. 154-6.

22 A. Ubersfeld, editor, Victor Hugo, Théâtre, I., op. cit., p. 878.

23 Ibid.

24 Ibid., p. 945.

25 Ibid., p. 946.

26 Ibid., p. 957.

27 Letter to F. M. Piave from G. Verdi in F. Abbiati, Verdi, Ricordi, Milan, 1959, p. 62.

28 See G. Cesaria and A. Luzio, editors, I copia-lettere di G. Verdi, Stucchi Ceretti, Milan, 1913, p. 487.

29 Ibid., pp. 489-90. For information regarding the life and reputation of Francis I of France, see: C. Osborne, Rigoletto – A guide to the Opera, Barrie and Jenkins, London, 1979.

30 For some basic background information on the Italian Commedia dell'Arte, see: P.L. Duchartre, The Italian Comedy (translated by R.T. Weaver, Dover/New York, 1966); C. Oreglia, The Commedia dell'Arte, Methuen, London, 1968; M. Apollonio, Storia della Commedia dell'Arte, Sansoni, Florence, 1982; F. Taviani and M. Schino, Il Segreto della Commedia dell'Arte, Casa Usher, Florence, 1982; C. Molinari, La Commedia dell'Arte, Mondadori, Milan, 1985; F. Marotti and G. Romei, La Commedia dell'Arte e la società barocca: la professione del teatro, Bulzoni, Rome, 1991.

31 G. Verdi, Rigoletto, Ricordi, Milan, p. 7. 1983.

32 Ibid., p. 16.

33 Ibid., p. 33.

34 Ibid., p. 43.

35 For an account of the Accademia dell'Arcadia, see: W. Binni, L'Arcadia e il Metastasio, Sansoni, Florence, 1963; A. Piromalli, L'Arcadia: Storia e antologia della critica, Palumbo, Palermo, 1963; L. Caretti and G. Luti (editors), La letteratura italiana per saggi storicamente disposti: il Seicento e il Settecento, Mursia, Milan, 1972, pp. 321-41; W. Binni, Preromanticismo italiano, Latenza, Bari, 1974; M.T. Muraro (editor), Metastasio e il mondo musicale, Olschki, Florence, 1986.

36 Se piace ei lice: If it pleases it is permitted. T. Tasso, Aminta, Act I, 3.

37 G. Verdi, Rigoletto, op.cit., p. 8.

38 Ibid., p. 45.

24

39 Ibid., p. 15.
40 See L. Baldacci, *La musica in Italiano: Libretti d'opera dell'Ottocento*, Rizzoli, Milan, 1997, pp. 89-105.
41 G. Verdi, *Rigoletto*, op.cit., p. 9.
42 Ibid., p. 12
43 Ibid., p. 15.
44 Ibid., p. 19.
45 Ibid.
46 Ibid.
47 Ibid.
48 Ibid., p. 15.
49 L. Baldacci, *La musica in Italiano: Libretti d'opera dell'Ottocento*, Rizzoli, Milan, 1997, p. 104.
50 Ibid., p. 105.
51 G. Gronda/P. Fabbri, *Libretti d'opera italiana: dal Seicento al Novecento*, Mondadori (I Meridiani), Milan, 1997, p. 317.
52 G. Verdi, *Rigoletto*, op.cit., p. 21.
53 Ibid.
54 Ibid., p. 40.
55 Ibid., pp. 48-9.
56 See C. Dapino (editor), *Il teatro italiano*, V, *Il libretto del melodramma dell'Ottocento*, II, Introduction by F. Portinari, Einaudi, Turin, 1984, pp. XXXVIII – XLI. For a general consideration of the combination of genres in Verdi, see: P. Weiss, 'Verdi e la fusione dei generi,' in L. Bianconi (editor), *La drammaturgia musicale*, Il Mulino, Bologna, 1986, pp. 75-92.
57 G. Verdi, *Rigoletto*, op.cit., p. 49.
58 Ibid., p. 61. Verdi himself considered the opera 'revolutionary'. See: F. Abbiati, Verdi, II, op.cit., p. 110.
59 Ibid., p. 47.
60 Ibid., p. 62.
61 M. Lavagetto (editor), *A. Boito, Opere*, Garzanti, Milan, 1979, p. 3.

CHAPTER 2

Duality: Art and Science in Arrigo Boito's
Il libro dei versi – Re Orso

In the wake of Italian unification, following the collective national pursuit of a single identity, in search of a political ideal, a sense of anti-climax pushed artists towards the acceptance of a new social ethos. Aspiration and revolution had carried the romantic dream towards reality. Unity and uniformity had utilized, as its mouthpiece, the Foscolian projection of art and the artists in the service of the nation in *Le ultime lettere di Jacopo Ortis* (1802) and the Manzonian identification of history and truth in *I promessi sposi* (1825-7,'42). While Foscolo chose contemporary events in order to illustrate the progression of history, Manzoni found his social message by exploring institutions and events of the baroque era. Foscolo's religion evolved as an artistic expression of patriotism. Manzoni's search for the sublime resulted in the personification of reason and revelation through the figure of Lucia. Manzoni's journey, and its philosophical, theological and linguistic significance, is communicated by means of a variety of literary devices ranging from satire, parody, the mock-heroic to the allegorical undercurrent which pervades the novel. Not all of Manzoni's followers and imitators grasped the complexity of his work. Nonetheless, the co-existence of the sublime alongside the ridiculous, and the comic figure of Don Abbondio as the source of a succession of serious events, places Manzoni on the path towards Modernist thought and expression. Interpreted as *caposcuola* of Romanticism, in the light of this study, he can be regarded as one who 'stands his ground' between two eras: the spectacle of pre-unification Italy and its deconstruction by the writers and artists who later came to be known as the 'Scapigliati'.[1]

Detailed attention has already been given to Piave's absorption of Hugo's dramatization of deformity and his preoccupation with the grotesque.[2] In 1851, this reflected the strong influence of French drama on Italian opera or *melodramma*. It emerged as a spontaneous elaboration of Hugo's key ideas, with musical and visual aids. With the dawning of the 1860's, the trend is continued by a more calculated and determined approach. With the passing of the 'beautiful' and 'harmonious' there is born the cult of the 'ugly'. Evil replaces Good as the subject of close analysis. Evil also is presented as the *subject* and *means* of scientific scrutiny. The cult of unity of form within the work of art, which was seen to have served a society with little in common with the post- unification reality, was overturned. The concept of 'form' gives way to 'deformity', as a new approach to image evolves. Such an image is the child of Science, the result of an analytical dissection of the subject matter, leading to its reconstruction. There follows the creation of the grotesque. As art is critically analyzed, it is destroyed, in order to give birth to a scientific exposition of its content. Art (in the works of Arrigo Boito) is represented by a poem, a corpse, a mummy, a torso. The contemplation of these forms, leads to a scientifically orientated act of reconstruction. This scientific exercise is ART in its new form. In its early stages (as will be illustrated by the works of Arrigo Boito) this is totally rational. Science and Reason go hand in hand. However, as the invention becomes more sophisticated it enters the realm of the fantastic, so destroying scientific principles on which constructed and resulting in the irrationality of the fantastic.[3] At this point we have reached Pirandello's *Il berretto a sonagli*. When considered in this light, the entire process is self annihilating. Yet there remains an Ars Nova, the absurdity of which resides in its combination of opposites. To this, we may conclude, Hugo's hunchback ultimately leads. The process is given formal poetic expression by the movement now known as Scapigliatura Milanese.[4]

As this chapter is principally concerned with the poetic compositions of Arrigo Boito, and the application of the theory contained therein in the libretto *Otello*, references to Scapigliatura will be limited to their relevance to this subject. The movement was born as an anti-bourgeois, bohemian conviction, that the artistic ethos and social conventions leading to the unification of Italy were outmoded and no longer pertinent to artistic creative expression. It determined and superimposed a set of 'non-values' which were juxtaposed with traditional, orthodox views, in order to surprise and shock. G. Mariani in his study *La Scapigliatura*,[5] has made the distinction between two stages of the movement: the 'prima' or first Scapigliatura expressed artistic and cultural aspirations, the second or democratic Scapigliatura was preoccupied with socio-political matters. While contemporaries failed to appreciate its importance, it is now accepted that it represented the first 'modern' school of Italian literature and a rediscovery of Evil, which to quote Rodolfo Quadrelli 'was not open to correction either by social reforms or scientific progress.'[6] The outstanding members of those advocating literary innovation were Emilio Praga (1839-75), Iginio Ugo Tanchetti (1839-69) and Arrigo Boito (1842-1918). They sought to identify literature with the figurative arts and music. In this respect they followed in the footsteps of the French bohemians, who were given artistic life by Henri Murger in the work *Scènes de la vie de Bohéme* (1847-9). This projects a series of scenes from a life free of convention, in the garrets of the Latin Quarter in Paris. It however represented a *lifestyle* as opposed to the experimentation with form and content, which the Italians drew from the work of Baudelaire, De Musset and Hoffmann. The Italianization of the term 'bohéme' occurred with the use of the word Scapigliatura by Cletto Arrighi as part of the title of his novel *La Scapigliatura e il 6 febbraio*,[7] the introduction to which had appeared four years previously in *Il pungolo*. The preface contains an analysis of the term and its social implications.[8] The 'scapigliati' are identified with the hope, idealism and revolutionary passion of youth and with the dissipation and desperation to which such enthusiasm and fervour can lead. Already one is aware of a duality of attitude and of how the source of Boito's 'dualismo' will span the period *Le roi s'amuse* (1831) and Murger's *Scènes de la vie de Bohéme* (1847-9) to the era of Milanese social revolt of the early 60's. The unrest, contradictions and antitheses found in Boito's work and sublimated in the libretto *Otello* for Giuseppe Verdi, is played out in the tragic lives of the members of the Milanese group: the death of Tarchetti from tuberculosis at the age of twenty nine, Praga's early demise as a result of drugs and alcohol aged thirty six and Camerana's suicide at the age of sixty. Boito, effectively is the survivor of Scapigliatura, whose cult of the ugly and the intellectualisation of the progress of Evil gives way to an unresolved antithesis, and link between form and content and Art and Science. In Boito's work the intellectual dimension will contrast and surpass the physical, while authors with more concentrated realist tendencies focus on the objective, the actual and the ugly. An example of this is Tarchetti's introduction of his protagonist in *Fosca* and his insistence of the ugliness of her physical appearance:

Dio! Come esprimere colle parole la bruttezza orrenda di quella donna!
Come vi sono beltà di cui è impossibile il dare un'idea,

così vi sono bruttezze che sfuggono ad ogni manifestazione, e tale era la sua. Né tanto era brutta per difetti di natura, per disarmonia di fattezze... per la rovina che il dolore fisico e le malattie avevano prodotto sulla sua persona ancora così giovane.[9]

U. Tarchetti, *Fosca* Ch. XV.

(God! How can one express in words the terrible ugliness of that woman! Just as there are forms of beauty, of which it is impossible to convey an idea, so there are types of ugliness that defy description, and such was hers. It was not so much that she was ugly on account of her natural defects – on account of disharmony of form...Rather because of the wear and tear that physical suffering and illness had placed on her body, still so young.)

Here one would appear to witness the disintegration of form, symbolized by the human body as opposed to the *deconstruction* and *reconstruction* of the object found in Boito. This latter process will occupy the central section of this chapter. The destructive processes as seen in Boito's works may be caused by social or physical violence or by the annihilation of an object in the service of Science.

Boito's *Il libro dei versi* (1877) consists of sixteen poems written between 1862 and 1867 and published in various periodicals.[10] It may be said that each contains the negative aspirations, to and definitions of ideals, in addition to an inner schizophrenia and contrasting associations of light and shade, real and ideal, good and evil. Of these poems I believe six to be particularly pertinent to this study. These are: 'Una mummia' (1862), 'Dualismo' (1864), 'Lezione d'anatomia' (1865), 'Case nuove' (1866), 'Madrigale' (1866) and 'Un torso' (1862). Since 'Dualismo' contains the basic opposing images found throughout Boito's poetic and prose works, it is a fitting introduction to a detailed consideration of the writer's intellectual progressions. 'Dualismo' first appeared in the *Figaro* of February 18th. 1864, and later in the *Strenna Italiana* of 1872. The poem consists of sixteen stanzas each containing seven lines. The rhyme scheme is ABCBDDE. It contains all the essential components of his later work: the ambiguous co-existence of opposites within the self, allied to the eternal transition of the individual between two states: that of sin and virtue. Never still, the poet is eternally searching for an ideal state as he walks a tightrope between light and shade, good and evil, while absorbed in active contemplation.

30

Son luce ed ombra, angelica
Farfalla o verme immondo,
Sono un caduto chèrubo
O un demone che sale
affaticando l'ale
Verso un lontano ciel.[11]
'Dualismo', l. 1-7.

(I am light and shade; an angelic butterfly
or a filthy worm. I am a fallen cherub, damned to
wander on earth, or a devil rising, winging
wearily towards a far distant sky.)

Straight away Boito, in the projection of the self, provides abstractions – light and shade, to illustrate not only the symbolic imagery of being, but also to provide a scientific undercurrent, which later in his work will develop and present a further duality or ambiguity. Light is reason, intellect and Science. Shade is created by light in darkness.[12] Later in the poet's progression, of ideas, one will question the permanent goodness of light – this will be the case in the 'Lezione d'anatomia' when Boito derides Science and learning and advocates a return to spontaneity. The concept of movement through space is conveyed early in the poem: 'caduto cherubo'/fallen angel, 'demone che sale'/rising devil, who pursues an ambition, beating his wings towards a *distant* sky/heaven. In this first stanza Boito concentrates on the creation of a double image: angel/devil. In the second stanza he creates his impression, not through the medium of vision, but that of hearing, as he expresses a thought within the mind:

Ecco perchè nell'intime
Cogitazioni io sento
La bestemmia dell'angelo.[13]
'Dualismo' l. 8-10.

(This is why in my deep meditations I hear the curse of the angel.)

The order of being is linked to the order of understanding. Here is a reversal of the Cartesian concept, 'I think therefore I am'. Boito's self *is* light and shade, and this is why he hears, *from within* the mind, as opposed to from without. He *is*, therefore he thinks and hears. It is because of *what* rather than *who* he is that he is intrigued and tormented by the conflicting forces which combine to create the whole:

> Ecco perchè m'affascina.
> L'ebbrezza di due canti.[14]
> 'Dualismo' l. 15-16.

> (This is why I am fascinated
> by the intoxication of two songs.)

With references to light and shade, and the insistence on the effect of being on the senses, Boito, up to this point in the poem is utilizing principles governed by physics. In the following stanza he expresses the possibility that his being may be pre-determined by chemical experimentation.

> Forse noi siam *l'homunculus*
> D'un chimico demente,
> Forse di fango e foco
> Per ozïoso gioco
> Un buio Iddio ci fe'.[15]
>
> 'Dualismo' l. 31-5.

> (Perhaps we are the scientific
> creations of a mad chemist.
> Perhaps, a dark god made us
> out of fire and mud,
> in order to ease his boredom.)

Having introduced Science as his possible essence and origin, Boito, now turns to Art, indicating that in reality his 'Dualismo' is the duality of Science and Art. In this poem there is no open conflict between the two, rather as will be indicated, in its closing lines, good and evil and their attributes alternate, with neither gaining the upper hand and uniting in 'duality'.

E sogno un'Arte eterea
Che forse in ciel ha norma
Franca dai rudi vincoli
Del metro e della forma,
Piena dell'Ideale
Che mi fa batter l'ale
E che seguir non so.[16]

'Dualismo', l. 77-83.

(And I dream of/aspire to an eternal Art
That perhaps in heaven has its rules.
Free of the coarse chains of metre and form.
Full of the Ideal
Which makes me beat my wings
And go I don't know where.)

Art cultivated as an Ideal is that for which the poet searches. Yet it must exist outside of structure, restriction and preconceived form. This is the reason for the poet's sense of confusion and lack of direction. Such a concept, is merely an ideal, since any reality or actual realization demands a form or anti-form hitherto undefined. It is however an ideal, taking the form of rebellion in order to distract the orthodox traditionalists. For Boito the latter are angels, having contemplated and cultivated the now accepted harmonious order. If such novelty or rebellion distracts the purists from their 'santi sogni' (pious dreams) l.86. then the poet states that he is carried away by this new light, on a changed horizon:

Allor, davanti al raggio
Del mutato miraggio
Quasi rapito sto. [17]

'Dualismo', l. 82-4.

(Then before the ray
of the changed mirage
I am almost carried away.)

Very quickly the dream of 'Arte eterea' (ethereal art), is replaced by 'Arte reproba' (rebellious art). It directs the poet's thoughts towards images that lie to the absolute truth, and inspire words of blasphemy:

> E sogno un'Arte reproba
> Che smaga il mio pensiero
> Dietro le basse imagin
> D'un ver che mente al Vero.
> E in aspro carme immerso
> Sulle mie labbra il verso
> Bestemmiando vien. [18]
>
> 'Dualismo', l. 92-8.

> (And I dream of/aspire to a rebellious ART.
> That makes my thought lose itself,
> Behind the low images of a truth
> Which lies to Truth,
> And immersed in an ugly poem
> The verse, blaspheming comes to my lips.)

Here two art-forms are in conflict: the ideal, and the real, the conventional and the rebellious. The 'duality' is within ART. The 'good', in the moral sense, is the ideal. The 'evil' is the rebellious. Yet the 'heavenly art' l. 77-83, perceived as being devoid of structure and form is in itself rebellious and revolutionary.[19] In the process of expressing his thoughts Boito has clarified his intention and has effectively created a poem of *contestazione* or protest. One may conclude that 'Dualismo' is Boito's Scapigliatura manifesto, containing as it does the cultivation of the forces of light and darkness, of scientific principles in order to define the self and justify his protest. Equilibrium is however achieved within the poem. An external alternation of light and shade, Science and Art, convention and rebellion is conveyed. The final metaphor is of a tightrope artist, performing before a crowd, and succeeding in maintaining his balance. Boito associates 'l'uman' (the human race) with the individual who performs feats of equilibrium. He no longer refers to the self in the first person singular or plural. Rather he has conferred universality on his dilemma. What had begun with the words: *Son luce ed ombra; angelica/far-*

falla o verme immondo/ indicating what he is, concludes with an illustration of human destiny, suspended between two dreams:

> Tale è l'uman, librato
> Fra un sogno di peccato
> E un sogno di virtù.[20]
> > 'Dualismo', l.110-12

> (Such is the human being,
> balanced between a dream of sin
> And a dream of virtue.)

'Dualismo' is a realistic extension of the metaphysical and philosophical questions raised in the first chapter on Piave's *Rigoletto*. Science has been introduced as both a means towards self-awareness and an all powerful force. Boito's poem has not confronted or contrasted the two sources of inspiration: the scientific and artistic. Rather he has allowed them work hand in hand, creating a poem full of spontaneous enthusiasm and astute, methodological progression.

An attempt to identify poetry with music and the figurative arts is registered in the eight line poem 'Madrigale' (Madrigal) of 1866. The information that the lines were written under a photographic portrait of the Duchess E...L... is provided as a subtitle. At once one grasps the poet's intention: the presentation of a concept of portraiture, not effected with the artist's brush, but rather in terms of a reproduction of reality, photographic reality, achieved by alternation of light and shade. The world of 'Dualismo', has been transported from its timeless setting, to serve a new scientific invention, the camera, the mastery of which combines Art and Science and requires technique and artistic appreciation.[21] The 'foto-ritratto' represents reality in a manner which can never be applied to the artist's portrait. In place of the painter's reproduction of nature, one is faced with the achievement of Science. The piece consists of two alternate stanzas of hendecasyllables and septenaries with the metre ABAB. The impression is of a short musical composition. The poem opens with a reference to the art of photographic portraiture as one born of light and poison:

> Arte nata da un raggio e da un veleno. [22]
> > 'Madrigale', l.1.

(Art born of light and poison)

The poet marvels at the combination of light and shade but would appear to juxtapose the ideal and the real, the artistic and scientific in the final lines:

> Sento il raggio negli occhi
> E il veleno nel core. [23]
>
> 'Madrigale', l. 7-8

> (I feel the light in my eyes
> And the poison in my heart.)

Duality represents, not only a series of antitheses, and unity forged through the association of opposites, but more significantly it contains a scientific approach to the self and to the interpretation of Art. It also stands as a prime example of a new art form, appealing as it does to the mind and to the intellect, rather than to the heart. 'Madrigale' does not refer to the 'object', the invention of which carries the new 'artistic technology' into the second half of the nineteenth century. Yet he expresses the effect of its presence. In 'Case nuove' (New Houses), of the same year (1866), Boito responds to another phenomenon of his day: the modernization of Milan as Luigi Baldacci states in *Poeti minori dell'Ottocento*, vol. I, p. 908. Boito being the brother of an architect, was informed of the new ventures in town planning effected at the time. Boito combines diverse rhyme schemes in order to create the chaos created by the sounds of instruments of destruction and demolition engaged in rebuilding the city and effectively creating a new modern world. A possible source is the poem *Demolitions* by Louis Bouilhet.

The 'duality' is here contained in the nostalgic recreation of the past by means of references to the world of nature, classical mythology and domestic simplicity. In addition Boito relies on images of light and darkness to demonstrate, by means of antithesis, that the new world is bright, white and that it expels the shades of deceased family members.[24] But paradoxically, in this setting of stark light symbolizing reality, the blind man will lose his way as he gropes and searches for direction. He appears as one who dreams. What would seem to be symbolic of a new civilization, heralds the end of the old forms which will be replaced by those of emptiness and materialism:

36

Sorge ogni giorno qualche casa bianca. 25

          'Case Nuove', l.7

(Every day some white houses appear)

Gia gli augelletti fidi
Più non trovano i nidi
Consueti fra il tetto, e la grondaia. 26

          'Case Nuove', l.18-20

(Already the faithful little birds
No longer find their usual nests, between
The roof and the gutter)

Fuggono l'ombre de'cari
Defunti .

          'Case Nuove' l. 24.5

(The shades of the dear deceased flee.)

E il cieco brancolante in sulla sponda
Della contrada – smarrirà la strada
Com'uom che sogna. 27

          'Case Nuove', l. 32-4.

(And the blind man groping along the boundary
Of the district – will lose his way
Like a man in a dream.)

The new social system, dominated by scientific and economic progress is parodied by Boito in 'A una mummia' (To a Mummy). As a result of Science a human form becomes a work of Art. For a modern world, it symbolizes a bygone civilization. It lives eternally, a living death, but it will come to life on the day of judgement, when it will free itself from its burial place. Unlike in the traditional image of the resurrection, the mummy will smash the glass of the display case in which it is exhibited.

The poem was written as a result of Boito's visit to the Egyptian Museum in Turin, in 1862. However the subject of embalming was a popular one in the works of the Scapigliati. Carlo Dossi pays homage to it in *Note Azzurre*.[28] Boito's work may have been influenced by 'La plainte d'une Momie' by Louis Bouilhet. If one accepts that the strongest influence on the Scapigliati came from France through Hugo, Murger, Baudelaire and Bouilhet, one might also argue that Boito continually builds on the ideas contained in his sources, inverts them, deconstructs and recreates. From the concept of the grotesque through deformity, Boito *preserves* ('A una Mummia'), *destroys* ('Case nuove'), *dissects* ('Lezione d'anatomia') and *recreates* ('Un torso') form.[29] The errors of nature represented by Triboulet and Quasimodo, are the sources of a new experimentation, with the tragedy of the grotesque descending to mere parody. 'A una mummia' demonstrates the preservation of a natural form, which becomes an 'object d'art' inspiring both admiration and ridicule.

In this poem, Boito is at his most artificial. The first image conveys the dual quality of the exhibit. Although its appearance is unnatural, it carries details of a life lived in a distant civilization:

> Mummia fasciata in logori
> Papiri sontuosi,
> Mummia che sul sudario
> Porti l'apoteosi. [30]
>
> 'A una mummia', l. 1-4

> (Mummy swathed in worn,
> Precious papyrus,
> Mummy, that on your shroud,
> Carry your apotheosis.)

The duality is continued, with reference to the place of origin of the Mummy and its contrast with the cold, damp climate of Northern Italy. Boito's precise choice of expression 'fulgido/Sole del tuo deserto' (the bright sun of your desert),[31] juxtaposed with 'gel d'un aer piorno (the freezing cold of the damp air), touches the senses of the reader. This in turn is contrasted with the communication of time and movement through continuity of rest and progress:

A così bella pace
Ti derubò rapace
Una che non ha posa
Scienza curiosa. [32]

'A una mummia', l. 21-4

(From such a beauteous peace,
You were greedily taken,
By one who
knows no rest,
Ever curious Science.)

As scholars study the historical worth of this pathetic object, we are reminded that its unnatural appearance provokes nightmares:

E nel guardarti il pargolo
S'asconde per paura,
Poi, nella notte orribile
Sogna la tua figura. [33]

'A una mummia', l. 49-52

(And the child, seeing you, hides in fear
And, later, in the horrible night
Dreams of your image.)

As in 'Lezione d'anatomia', Boito muses on the emotions which this mute creature must have felt. As a result of the sad expression on the face of the mummy, it is obvious that it once contained a soul. Boito conveys his intuition in terms of words appartaining to sound: 'Sorda testa' (deaf head), 'Lo sento' (I hear it). He then alternates what he senses and hears, with what the mummy heard, and felt, thus artificially carrying its past emotions, to the present. Boito builds his climax by emphasizing the human qualities of the mummy. He then introduces gentle humour: as an eternal observer of social change, it will never change. It will continue to see through dead eyelids. Time will have no effect on it:

E il tempo che ne fruga

Non segnerà una ruga

Sovra il tuo volto scarno

E freddo come marmo. [34]

'A una mummia', l. 85-8.

(And the passing of time,

Which torments us,

will not show a line

on your gaunt face

Cold as marble.)

When time shall become eternity, on the day of the Last Judgement, the mummy instead of rising from the dead, shall finally break out of its glass prison:

Mummia, quella mattina

Romperai la vetrina. [35]

'A una mummia', l. 95-6

(Mummy on that morning

you will break the glass case.)

The destiny of the mummy is different from that of mankind: rather than *be* liberated, it will *liberate itself*. Science will return to Nature, and find again a natural form. While in 'Lezione d'anatomia' Science is exalted, only later to be dismissed, in 'A una mummia', it is parodied. It gives birth to a lifeless form, which will be returned to nature by the supernatural. One is here aware of the germs of *Mefistofele*. Faust as the chemist and object of experimentation, pales before the superhuman Mefistofele. Yet I believe that in this poem Boito wishes to strip Science of any philosophical attribute. It has not managed to preserve a living form, or create the 'homunculus' of 'Dualismo'. Rather it has displayed a curiosity in order to satisfy its own needs.

In 'Un torso' Boito attempts to restore to its origins what Art has created and society has destroyed. The 'torso', once a Venus, chiselled to beauteous perfection is without a head. It no longer contains the physical receptacle of thought, yet the mind of the artist succeeds in expressing its intentions through the torso. The result is the incongruous combination of the abstract thoughts and intentions of the artist and the remaining form of Venus. Mind and matter are thus joined. The poet detaches himself from the contemplation of the image to return to the ancient world, in order to provide the history of the object and its evolution through Greek, Roman and Modern civilization. Until the final stanza 'Il torso' develops as a confrontation of Nature and Art, and the moulding of the natural into the artistic and artificial. Tribute is paid to the piece of marble, highlighted by the half-light of dawn and dusk. Art artificially forms the Venus, and constructs a civilization to highlight and display such perfect female forms.

> Poi t'ebbe Roma, emporio
> Di statue e di colonne,
> Teatro allor di Veneri
> Com'oggi di Madonne. [36]
>
> 'Il torso', l.73-6.

> (Then Rome emporium of statues
> and columns, got possession of you.
> Then a theatre of Venuses
> As today one of Madonnas.)

The violence and decadence of Roman society finally causes the destruction of the form. Further violence is threatened by the restorers, who seek to replace the arms of the Venus. In the poem Art & Nature finally become the captives of Science, which seeks to imprison and improve, by forced completion and reconstruction. In many respects, the poem bears similarities to 'A una mummia' in so far as it takes its point of departure from the contemplation of an 'objet d'art', imprisoned in the museum. Boito wrote the poem following a visit to the Louvre in 1862. The essential difference between the two works is that while the 'Mummy' is the result of a scientific process of preservation, the 'Torso' has fallen victim to the destructive forces of time and social abuse.

In the poem Boito succeeds in combining two styles: the comical, leading to parody, and the serious. Parody is utilized in the service of precision of statement, and in contrasting the lifeless with life. The following lines illustrate the point:

41

Di tant'arte non resta
Che un busto senza testa. [37]

'Un torso', l. 7-8.

(Of such art, there remains
But a bust devoid of a head

....

Pur colle rotte braccia
Quel torso ancor m'allaccia. [38]

'Un torso', l. 21-2.

(Yet with its broken arms
That torso still embraces me.)

Con un osceno crollo
T'hanno fiaccato il collo. [39]

'Un torso', l. 87-88.

(With an obscene blow,
They broke your neck.)

Such lines highlight the incomplete nature of the subject, while providing a 'send up' of the source of its fame and possible restoration. The final lines contain the surprise element favoured by Boito in 'A una mummia' and 'Lezione d'anatomia'. This is emphasized, as we are reminded by Quadrelli, with the placing of a dieresis on the 'a' of 'Restäuratore, which has the effect of slowing the final line:

Oggi forse minaccia
Quelle tue monche braccia
Di più fiero dolore:
Il restäuratore.[40]

'Un torso', l. 109-112.

(Perhaps today,
the restorer threatens

your incomplete arms,
with further cruel pain.)

In the poems under scrutiny, Boito appears to both venerate and deride Art and to demonstrate the necessary co-existence of Art and Science, yet he ridicules the latter to the extent that one must accept that Boito's vision of the world, and its constituents is ironic. Irony leads to parody, devoid of humour. There is a final shock effect in 'A una mummia, 'Un torso', 'Lezione d'anatomia', which destroys the logical progression and the calculated imagery created in the course of each work. In the highly successful 'Lezione d'anatomia', Boito's entire technique and poetic philosophy is unveiled. Scientific dissection leads to his veneration of his artistic ideal, which he consequently destroys by referring to the real. In an anatomy theatre, at dawn, the body of a young girl is the subject of an anatomy lesson. She is a double victim, of fate and of Science. As her form is dissected, the doctor roars out his lesson with positive conviction. As the actual and scientific dominate, Boito muses on the dreams and appearance of the youthful beauty, and bids Science to depart, in order to be replaced by dreams and ideals. The young girl is ART and is addressed as the sweet, pure, languishing flower of poetry. As the poetic work of art, she is dissected and analysed, not in the service of artistic criticism, but scientific progress. Life and death are juxtaposed, and the nineteenth-century positivist dialogue between Nature and Science is introduced. Where all ends for Nature in death, it is born for Science. Nature's death is the life of Science. Boito carries the conflicting dualism a step further: as he contemplates the purity of innocence of the adolescent, the professor discovers a thirty day foetus. The dream perishes in the face of reality. The promise of new life, in a dead body cannot be fulfilled. Thus the possibility of new life is both introduced and negated, with the death of its source. Yet, the subject of dissection is poetry: killed of its spontaneity by the scientific principles which govern it and to which it must conform: destroyed and rendered lifeless by an analytical approach which negates its subject matter and lyricism.

The fate of the body after death has been discussed in 'A una mummia'. Science has rendered it a work of art. Carlo Dossi, in *Note azzurre* also provides an anatomy lesson as does Praga in his poem 'A un feto' (To a foetus). Boito's 'Lezione d'anatomia' carries the date 1865. In 1870, Camillo Boito, Arrigo's older brother wrote 'Un corpo' (A body). "It too renders a similar world of morgues, hospitals, dissections and internal organs, and flagellates science".[41] It also disputes the dual role of art in a bourgeois society. However, as in many of the poems of Arrigo Boito's *Il libro dei versi*, parody carries the argument in the direction of decadence, as irony becomes comical, and results in the degradation of the subject i.e. 'A una mummia', 'Un torso'.

The poem opens as dawn *descends*, to reveal a sleeping corpse, deprived of funeral rites and religious consolation:

> La sala è lùgubre,
> Dal negro tetto
> Discende l'alba,
>
> Chi dorme?...un etica
> Defunta ieri,
> All'ospedale; [42]
>
> 'Lezione d'anatomia', l. 1-3, 7-9

> (The hall is gloomy,
> From the black roof
> Dawn descends
>
> Who sleeps?...a consumptive
> who died yesterday at the hospital.)

The image of the girl, pale in the darkness, provides the stark contrast between darkness and light. The image is bloodstained. The past is evoked in the *ritornello* of the poem:

> Ed era giovane!
> Ed era bionda!
> Ed era bella. [43]
>
> 'Lezione d'anatomia', l. 22-24

> (And she was young!
> And she was fairhaired!

And she was beautiful.)

Science and illness have not distorted or deformed the image of poetic beauty. Consumption, being the Romantic illness 'par excellence' carries with it the Romantic disposition of the poet. His response to the image of death, illness and violence is the contemplation of the mind and thoughts of the young girl:

> Io penso ai teneri
> Casi passati
> Su quella testa,
> Ai sogni estatici
> Invan sognati
> Da quella mesta. [44]
>
> > 'Lezione d'anatomia', l. 37-42.

> (I think of the tender happenings
> which passed through that head,
> of the estatic dreams,
> Dreamed in vain
> by that sad creature.)

As the image becomes increasingly poetic it becomes associated with ART. It is not yet poetry. Boito reconstructs an ideal, consisting of the real and its relationship to past dreams, without future fulfilment. Its thoughts are converted to the purer abstract form 'speranza' (hope) which is described as less permanent than a poetic stanza of four lines:

> Finzion fuggevole
> Più che una stanza
> Di quattro versi. [45]
>
> > 'Lezione d'anatomia' l. 46-8.

> (An invention more fleeting than
> a stanza of four lines.)

The poet identifies the mind with poetry, while the body continues to serve Science. The heart which had guarded its most sacred sentiments, is now exposed in its physiological detail:

> "Ecco le valvole",
> "Ecco le celle",
> "Ecco l'aorta." [46]
>> 'Lezione d'anatomia', l. 58-60.

> (Here are the valves
> Here are the cells
> Here is the aorta)

There follows Boito's most open dismissal of Science, and a return to ART, and to poetry symbolized by the young girl. The fleeting dream, identified with the 'Stanza of four lines', gives way to the languishing flower of poetry, which is her entire form and spirit:

> Scïenza, vattene
> Co' tuoi conforti!
> Ridammi i mondi
> Del sogno e l'anima!
> Sia pace ai morti
> E ai moribondi
>
> Pardona, o pallida
> Adolescente!
> Fanciulla pia,
> Dolce, purissima,
> Fiore languente
> Di poesia! [47]
>> 'Lezione d'anatomia', l. 67-78.

> (Begone Science,
> With your consolations

46

Give me back the worlds
Of dreams and of the spirit.
May peace be with the dead
And with the dying.

Pardon, o pale adolescent
Pious young girl,
Sweet, most pure
Languid flower
Of poetry)

With the discovery of the foetus, the spiritual ideal is destroyed, and it is replaced
by the real. Yet, within the thoughts evoked by the presence of the woman, real and
ideal co-exist and are bound together. They co-exist also within the poetic form
created by Boito, as do Nature, Science and Art. Unlike in the case of 'A una mummia' and 'Un torso', Boito does not resort to parody, irony or the grotesque. The
work develops as an exposition of the clinical and its juxtaposition with the sentimental. The body and the mind of the subject are exposed in contrasting poetic
styles: from that of dramatic exposition and statement, to tender recollection. The
young girl is both misfortune and the subject of forensic analysis, which aids new
poetic creativity as a result of her *physical* destruction.[48] Here is Boito's
'Dualismo' scored in a totally different register, yet no less effective. In place of
the 'Io' of self description and investigation of 'Dualismo', there is 'quella mesta',
(that sad one) with activity focused on the third person. One might suggest that if
'Dualismo' is about the Poet as the voice of mankind, then 'Lezione d'anatomia',
the scientific exposition of knowledge, is paradoxically about Poetry and all its
contradictory consituents. Within the confines of this work, Science is seen as violent, violating the privacy due to the dead and dying. Boito's choice of address to
Science: 'Scïenza Vattene' recalls the words of Christ 'Begone Satan'. Indirectly,
Science is the devil's advocate, utilizing beauty and youth in the pursuit of knowledge and ambition. Art however can confront, and contain such an exercise.

Boito published *Re Orso* in Milan in 1865 in *Strenna italiana*. Eight years later
it was publised again by Bona of Turin. A further edition was published by
Casanova of Turin in 1877 and finally, the authors definitive version by the same
publisher in 1902. An amount of variation between these editions can be noted.[49]

The edition of 1865 reveals Boito at his most angry and confrontational, and the numerous attacks on the Church and religious practice, illustrate the anti-literary and anti-conventional disposition of the 'Scapigliato'.[50] The subsequent editions[51] contain a toning down of the most open invectives against institutions, leading to a more subtle presentation of intent and ambiguity. Boito's need to continually revise his work is seen later in his career with *Mefistofele* and *Nerone*. The poem *Re Orso* represents the first stage of an established pattern. It was published in each of the editions cited (with the exception of that in *Strenna italiana*) along with *Il libro dei versi*. One notes a thematic relationship between the two. However, the aesthetic and scientific discourses on poetry descends to mere parody of their personifications, and in many respects the poem may be seen as a return to the grotesque and deformed, as seen in Victor Hugo. While Hugo, as we have seen in *Le roi s'amuse* dramatizes physical and moral deformity on a grand scale, Boito provides a temporal distancing resulting in the work shrinking in scale, and taking on the attribute of a puppet show.[52]

There have been many diverse interpretations of the poem and it is indeed difficult to provide a definitive account of its meaning. Giovanna Scarsi calls it a 'personification of 'Dualismo' ,[53] Rodolfo Quadrelli sees in it a re-evocation of Dante's Malebolge,[54] Benedetto Croce, in touching on its essence and the manner of its manifestation states: 'It is Evil: not conscious, timid, petty human Evil, but Evil as a manifestation of nature...This is poetry that borders on music![55] In 1875 Boito, described the work to Count Agostino Salina as 'Una matta cosa' (a crazy thing),[56] and urged him not to pass it around. Nonetheless he had furnished Verdi with a pre-publication copy in 1864, and around the same time sent a copy to Victor Hugo,who acknowledged a combination of 'the poetry of philosophy and chemistry'.[57] Hugo showed true enthusiasm for Boito, which further consolidates the linking of Hugo, Piave and Boito as the true Romantic realists, who paved the way for Modernism. Hugo, on 16 May 1866 wrote to Boito: 'Bravo, poet, there is a hero in you! You have courage. You have earned Venice. You shall have her, and Rome as well!' The letter refers to the exploits of Praga, Boito and Faccio in the war between Prussia and Austria, with the Scapigliati fighting on the side of the former for the liberation of Venice. However, the 'Venetian connection' will prove to be more significant when a closer look at the text of *Re Orso* is undertaken.

The legend of King Orso is as follows: the evil King of Crete, having decapitated his mistress, is offered in her place the personification of beauty and purity, the Venetian Oliba. With the aid of the snake Ligula, Orso rapes her, and from this point begins to hear warnings in his head to the effect: 'King Orso, protect yourself from the bite of the worms'. He hires a Jester, Papiol to locate the source of the voice, which he duly does, in a seal and a magpie. These are killed by the royal cook Trol, a giant. The song is perpetrated by a troubadour, who Papiol fails to eliminate. As his punishment he becomes the filling of a royal pie. Orso and Oliba marry. Their marriage is a death feast, attended by the King's twelve ministers, symbolizing the twelve apostles at the Last Supper of Christ. Oliba offers the king an apple containing a worm. In a fury, Orso beheads both Oliba and the worm. The voice of the troubadour is heard, but silenced by the impact created by Oliba's head, which comes crashing from the Palace window. One hundred years later Orso confesses to a corrupt friar. As the motif 'Re Orso/ti schermi/dal morso/de'vermi' consumes the King, he dies, and is eventually eaten by the worm, who makes a symbolic journey towards his corpse. The scene returns to the present: Orso's ghost travels the world taking the opposite direction of the sun, while the worm eats away at his palate and tongue.

The legend is divided into two sections: 'Orso vivo' (Orso alive) and 'Orso moto' (Orso dead). It is structured in a highly original manner: part one contains a preamble and six sections. The second part also contains six sections. The final section is dedicated to the moral of the piece. The poem's polymetric forms introduce episodes which have the effect of dramatic narrative: ancient tales, spectrum, a wedding. These alternate with the tales of the inhabitants of the Court of the King: Papiol the hunchback and dwarf, the troubadour and the giant Trol, who provide dialogue, speaking as they do, in the first person. These last mentioned create a sense of imbalance with regard to the visual impression projected i.e. the small and deformed contrasts with the gigantic. Through the troubadour, the chivalric world is introduced. This is anihilated by Oliba's head, which is flung from a window. One finds thus the re-construction of the world of the germanic fairytale complete with goblin, giant and knight. It is however robbed of its enchanted atmosphere by the ironic perversion of its function: it serves and aids the amoral as opposed to the good. An anti-fairy tale, then, in which the king is a monster, the heroine loses her head and continuity is provided by the appearance, journey and triumph of the worm.

Re Orso is a work about Evil in all its forms and aspects. It illustrates the higher and lower forms of Evil, through parody, resulting in the transformation of the beautiful to the absurd and ridiculous. It also degrades the world of Dante, Petrarch, Leopardi and Manzoni. At its conclusion its moral emerges: that there is no moral. It is a game of lotto, a mad tale of an executioner, a friar, a hunchback, a worm and a King.

As *Re Orso* has constantly been cited as Boito's most representative work, it is useful to forge a link between it and *Il libro dei versi* before proceeding to consider *Mefistofele* and *Otello*. The first section called *Esordio* (preamble) serves as a warning to religious bigots, young and old, that they fear 'la pagina orrenda' (the horrible page) of the legend about to unfold. Evil and Good are represented by Orso and Oliba and the enormity of the king's crimes is emphasized by the fact that his home is Crete, that of the Minotaur. His brute face and subhuman qualities are communicated in the Leggenda Prima – Storie Antiche (First Legend–Ancient Tales):

> La maledetta
> Per l'amor di Pasife isola infame,
> Terra di mostri e di delitti, aveva
> Re pari ad essa, ed era il Re nel nome
> Feroce a dirsi, al suo cuor pari: Orso[58]

> (The infamous island, cursed
> on account of the
> love of Pasife,
> A land of monsters and of crimes
> Had a king, its equal.
> And the king had a name,
> Ferocious in sound
> And equal to his heart: Orso)

Ferocity is associated with the animal kingdom. Orso's introduction coincides with the reference to Pasife and her copulation with a bull, resulting in the birth of the Minotaur of Crete. Orso however, was, it seems a common name during the Middle Ages. It was also the name of the military leader, who first assumed power in Venice, as a forerunner to the Doges. Oliba, not by coincidence I feel, is of Venetian origin. If one considers the twofold qualities of the Adriatic city: beauty and decay, one might thus explain Oliba's offering of the apple to Orso, complete with the worm of corruption and decay.[59] If the worm symbolizes Evil at is lowest level, then Orso, as its counterpart is the absolute, yet sub-human evil being. Since Evil is self consuming, Re Orso is finally devoured by the worm, ironically demonstrating that the greatest and most powerful creatures may be destroyed by the smallest and most insignificant ones.

Orso's crimes, and their immensity become identified with time, and time yields to space. The work, set in the Dark Ages, spans two centuries, thus proclaiming the duration of Evil. Although mindless, Orso suffers mental disturbance in the form of the voices proclaiming:

> Re Orso
> Ti schermi
> Dal morso
> De' vermi.

> (King Orso protect yourself
> of the bite of worms)

In an effort to expel such internal warnings, and destroy their sources, he decapitates both Oliba and the worm. In a search for peace of mind, the King decapitates and deforms. Orso, however, does not succeed in relieving *his* mental torment, by removing the head and destroying the mind and instinct of the symbols of Good and Evil. Paradoxically a sub-human, psychological drama is unfolding, moments of which can be clearly interpreted. However the relationship of these moments to the legend as a whole proves more difficult to establish.[60]

Throughout the poem in a variety of literary styles, ranging from the popular to the allegorical and lyrical, the form and content of canonical literary works are parodied. Such a device illustrates the acceptance by Boito of the author in question as part of literary history, which must be rejected, taken apart and reformed. In this respect *Re Orso* may be judged as destructive criticism. Its protagonist is the antithesis of ART, learning and civilization, in proximity to whom beauty and lyrical expression is dismembered, degraded and destroyed. It may be interpreted as a cry for a new ethos, a new society and a new myth of man.[61]

The king and his jester may well be parodies of Francis I and Triboulet of

Hugo's *Le roi s'amuse*.[62] In a battle between Orso (the bear) and the 'gobbetto' (hunchback dwarf), might conquers. Boito's use of the titles 'Orso vivo' and Orso morto', confronts the medieval convention of dividing poetic works into sections referring to the life and death of the subject i.e. Petrarca, *Il Canzoniere*: 'In vita di Madonna Laura, In morte di Madonna Laura'. Boito, then with regard to character (which fast becomes caricature) and form, accepts a convention which he quickly distorts, or for want of a better word, deforms. A strong example of this is his representation of the moon. Although introduced in Leopardian terms, it is transformed to a blind woman shedding light. As an infirm being she slowly makes her way across the sky. The following lines are a conscious evocation of 'La sera del di di festa':

> É scorsa un'ora, sulla terra bruna
> Vaga la luna – lenta incerta bieca,
> Come una cieca; – più non batton l'orme
> Dell'uom che dorme; – tutto è sonno, pace
> Il mondo tace; – sui caldi orizzonti
> S'ergono il monti – come gruppi vari
> Di dromedari.[63]

> (An hour has passed,The moon wanders
> On the brown earth
> Slow, uncertain, sinister
> Like a blind woman.
> The tracks of the sleeping man
> no longer sound. All is sleep and peace.
> The world is silent. The hills rise
> Like various groups of dromedaries.)

One might argue that these lines are not only an evocation of Leopardi, but also that they antithesize the Romantic poets perception of the moon as a purveyor of light, beauty and enlightenment. As a sinister blind woman, she steals across the sky, a witch rather than a goddess. Later in her rounded form she is made to resemble a musical note, synonymous with harmony. Yet, it must be borne in mind that the image of the note in manuscript form is black. Boito is carrying his 'Dualismo' towards the reorganization of literary and idealogical convention through image, poetry and the evocation of musical expression:

> E ancora la luna
> Splende sull'ermo
> Tonda ed immota
> Come una nota
> Di canto fermo.[64]

> (And still the moon
> shines on the solitary landscape
> Round and motionless
> As a note of steady song.)

There is, in the image of the moon, not only contrast, but also conflict and contradiction: she is 'incerta' (uncertain, or unsteady) in movement as a blind woman. With regard to image, she is compared to the steady emission of vocal tone. As a sound is emitted, it would seem to be that of a hoarse seal, carried on the wind as a lament, crying 'Re Orso/Ti schermi/Dal morso/De'vermi.'[65] Section 3 Litania is proclaimed by a Capuchin friar. It is a parody on the Litany of the Saints, naming devils, monsters, infernal guardians, damned heretical Popes, Manto Sibylla and closing with the words of Nembroth, the giant of Dante's *Inferno* XXXI.I.67. The entire form highlights moments from *Inferno*: Pape Satan (*Inferno* X), Pape Pluton (*Inferno* VII), Pape Caron (*Inferno* III), Gerion (*Inferno* X), Manto Sibylla (*Inferno* XI). The friar also calls on the anti-Christ and cities of perversion and lust i.e. Sodom, Gomorrah and Babylon, (the latter with political, papal and linguistic associations). The choice of Dantean references forming the Litany of the Damned, provides a further example of a hymn to Evil. The poetic replacement of the hitherto literary pursuit of order, harmony and esthetic values, by confusion, blasphemy and black comedy constitute a doctrine of denial and perversion.

Following the death of Re Orso, the motif of the worm is replaced by the image of a handsome Cretan knight, who arrives to participate at the funeral rites of the King. He is introduced with a lightness of tone which denies his claim to be Orso's ancestor:

O il bel cavaliero
Dal volto fatale
Dal magico vezzo.[66]

(Oh the handsome knight
of the fatal countenance
of the magical charms.)

On the disappearance of the Knight, the motif of the worm is re-introduced. Orso killed the worm, yet the worm did not die. Worms do not die, and at the moment of Orso's death, it begins its journey of revenge: The handsome knight and the headless worm represent a further 'duality': chivalry and corruption, which both react to the death of the King. The worm motif is now progressive, as opposed to repetitive. It is, as death, closer every day. It represents the passing of time and the inevitability of the end of the life span. But the logic of the progression is turned to ridicule: Orso is already dead. The function of the worm is to transform the corpse to nothingness.

E sera e mattina
Un verme cammina[67]

(And morning and evening
A worm walks.)

E il verme viaggia[68]
(and the worm travels)

It crosses the sea to Rhodes. Its journey is made lighter by the body of a cat, which provides food and passage.

E continuò il suo viaggio[69]
(and he continued his journey)

As the tale nears its conclusion, it enters the realm of the horror story. The active *symbol* of evil and corruption will reduce to nothing the remains of evil. The act of destruction will be complete. When one searches for the sources of the episode, Poe's *The Conqueror Worm* comes to mind, alongside Baudelaire's *La Charogne*. However, the journey of the worm may also represent a parody on Renzo's journey in Manzoni's *I promessi sposi*, 'Cammina cammina, trova cascine[70] (He continues to walk – he finds farmhouses). Renzo's journey symbolizes a movement away from the chaos of Milan, to the freedom of the Venetian Republic, by way of the River Adda, a boundary between good and evil, knowledge and ignorance. Renzo's journey is physical, moral and intellectual. As one engaged in a learning process, effected by activity, he symbolizes the active Everyman on the road to understanding. The worm's journey is not based on the breaking of new ground. It is one of return, and revenge. It does not seek to create, but rather to annihilate. The intellectual deductions are invited from the readers, since the worm, still without a head is incapable of rational thought. *Re Orso* then, is an intellectual journey towards Chaos, realistically unfolded in terms of a variety of metric forms, creating songs and airs in familiar liturgical tones. The 'morale', a declamation of no moral, but rather a 'strambo-quaderno' (a crazy *copy-book*), reinforces the belief that the work aims at creating an immense nothingness, completed by the worm and initiated by rape, denial, blasphemy, decapitation and destruction. It is a tale of 'Un boja e un frate, un gobbo, un verme e un re'.[71] (An executioner and a friar, a hunchback, a worm and a king). *Re Orso* has been published and consistently studied in conjunction with *Il libro dei versi*. A certain progression may indeed be established. Metric variety and contrasting poetic forms assume an increasing importance. Sound effect and refrain supersede imagery. The basic duality of *Il libro dei versi* is present. Any attempt however to intellectualize evil, results in the parody and degradation of conventional forms, summoned in the service of the central theme of the work. Art and Science do not here come into conflict, but rather do the sub-human and the beautiful. The protagonists are no more than symbolic objects, puppets controlled by a demented puppet-master, who sets up a battle between the conscious and the subconcious. In this respect, Boito is setting his stage for the dramatization of opposites, in an art form containing words and music, where annhilation and destruction become creative forces.

In *Il libro dei versi*, Good and Evil are seen as complementary attributes of the man and the artist. Science and Art ultimately are reconciled in the poetic form. In *Re Orso* the contrasts are absolute and one might argue infantile. It is my belief that Boito has arrived at a stage in his career in which the word alone does not suffice to express the complexities of his vision: he must of necessity look to drama and to music-drama to complete his quest for innovation. One witnesses the deformity of both the poetic symbol and expression. The reconstruction of form and the creation of uniformity will be the result of adaptation, collaboration and poetic dramatization.

NOTES

1   See G. Farinelli, *Dal Manzoni all Scapigliatura*, Istituto Propaganda Libraia, Milan, 1991. For a definitive survey of the literature of a United Italy see: G. Tellini, *Il romanzo italiano dell'Ottocento e Novecento*, Bruno Mondadori, Milan, 1998, pp. 113-121.

2   See W. Kayser, *The Grotesque in Art and Literature*, Indiana University Press, Bloomington, 1963. Essential reading for the understanding of the genre is G. Gori, *Il grottesco nell'arte e nella letteratura. Comico, tragico, lirico*, Stock, Rome, 1926; *Scenografia: la tradizione e la rivoluzione contemporanea*, Stock, Rome, 1926. Also invaluable is P.D. Giovanelli's edition and commentary on Gori's works. See: P.D. Giovanelli, *Gino Gori: Il grottesco ed altri studi teatrali*, Bulzoni, Rome, 1978.

3   For an introduction to the theory of the fantastic see: N. Bonifazi, *Teoria del fantastico e il racconto fantastico in Italia: Tarchetti, Pirandello, Buzzati*, Longo, Ravenna, 1982.

4   For basic backrground reading on the Scapigliatura see: P. Nardi, *Scapigliatura Da Giuseppe Rovani a Carlo Dossi*, Zanichelli, Bologna, 1924 now, Mondadori, Milan, 1968; G. Mariani, *La Scapigliatura*, Sciascia, Caltanisetta-Rome, 1967; F. Bettini, *La critica e gli scapigliati*, Zanichelli, Bologna 1976; G. Scarsi, *Scapigliatura e Novecento*, Stadium, Rome, 1979; A. Sozzi-Casanova, *La Scapigliatura*, Cooperativa Libreria, I.V.L.M., Milan, 1979; D. Isella, 'Approccio all Scapigliatura', in I *Lombardi in rivolta*, Einaudi, Turin, 1984, pp. 231-9; I. Crotti/R. Ricorda, *Scapigliatura e dintorni (Storia letteraria d'Italia)*, vol. 10, *L'Ottocento*, Vallardi, Milan, c. 1992; D. Del Principe, *Rebellion, Death and Aesthetics in Italy. The Demons of Scapigliatura*, Associated University Presses, New York, 1996; G. Rosa, *La narrativa degli Scapigliati*, Laterza, Roma-Bari, 1997.

5   G. Mariani, *La Scapigliatura*, Sciascia, Caltanisetta-Rome, op.cit.

6   See R. Quadrelli (editor), *Arrigo Boito, poesie e racconti*, Mondadori, Milan, 1981, p.7.

7   The work has as its setting the unsuccessful Mazzinian rising of 1853. In its second edition the title of the novel is: *La Scapigliatura. Romanzo sociale contemporaneo* (1880). See: G. Farinelli, editor, *La Scapigliatura. Romanzo sociale contemporaneo*, Istituto Propaganda Libraria, Milan, 1978; R. Fedi (editor), *La Scapigliatura e il 6 febbraio (Un dramma in famiglia) Romanzo contemporaneo* (1862), Mursia, Milan, 1988.

8   Although Arrighi does not acknowledge the influence of Murger's preface to *Scènes de la vie de Bohème* (1847-9), the former's preface is modelled on the French novelist's structure and form. See: A. Sozzi–Casanova, *La Scapigliatura*, op.cit., pp. 8-11.

9   See I.U. Tarchetti, *Fosca*, in E. Ghidetti (editor) *Tutte le opere*, Cappelli, Bologna, 1967, 2, vol. II, pp. 277-8. In his study *Il romanzo italiano dell'Ottocento e Novecento*, Mondadori, Milan, 1998, p. 122, Tellini makes a comparison with Verga's *Nedda* (1874), so linking the anti-Romanticism of Scapigliatura, to Verga's *Vinti*. Many other of the Sicilian author's heroines come to mind: La Rossa (*Pane Nero*, 1883), Diodata and Bianca (*Mastro-don Gesualdo*).

10 See R.De Rensis, *Lettere di Arrigo Boito*, Società Editrice 'Novissima', Rome, 1932; P. Nardi (editor), *Arrigo Boito,Tutti gli scritti*, Mondadori, Milan, 1942; M. Lavagetto (editor), *Boito, opere*, Garzanti, Milan, 1979, Introduction pp. V-xxxviii; R. Quadrelli (editor), *Arrigo Boito, Poesie e racconti*, Mondadori, Milan, 1981, Introduction pp. 5-25. For further critical study see: A. Pompeati, *Arrigo Boito, poeta e musicista*, Battistelli,   Florence, 1919; C. Ricci, Arrigo Boito, Trevès, Milan, 1924. V. Marini, *A Boito, Fra Scapigliatura e classicismo*, Loescher, Turin, 1968; *Le varianti di A. Boito, in Ottocento romantico e verista*, Naples, 1972, pp. 279-90; R. Giazotto, 'Hugo, Boito e gli scapigliati', originally in *L'approdo letterario*, Luglio-Settembre 1958 now in AA.VV. *L'opera italiana in musica*, Milan 1965. P. Nardi's *Arrigo Boito, Vita*, Mondadori, Milan, 1942 provides the essential socio-historical background to Boito's work.

11 See Rodolfo Quadrelli, *Arrigo Boito, poesie e racconti*, Mondadori, Milan, 1981, p. 39.

12 It would appear that Boito is aware of Leopardi's use of light metaphysics in order to provide an ambiguity of interpretation, where pure daylight indicates stark reality, while the shadow

conveyed by a glimmer of light in darkness conveys hope. This Leopardian ambiguity, becomes more apparent in his later poems: in 'La ginestra' and 'Il tramonto della luna'.

13 R. Quadrelli, *Arrigo Boito, Poesie e racconti*, op.cit., p. 39.

14 Ibid. Structurally the sentence also tends towards an amibiguity, although the meaning is perfectly clear. It could also read: I am intoxicated by the fascination of two songs.

15 Ibid., p. 40

16 Ibid., p. 41

17 Ibid., p. 42

18 Ibid.

19 It would appear from such conclusions, that Boito is incapable or unwilling to provide a totally objective and positivist view point. For this reason as also claimed by G. Petronio, *Dall'illuminismo al verismo*, Manfredi, Palermo, 1962, the Scapigliati cannot be regarded as realists, as their poetry is primarily concerned with the relative, and relationships between opposites. See also E. Sormani, *Bizantini e decadenti nell'Italia umbertino*, Laterza, Rome, 1975.

20 R. Quadrelli, Arrigo Boito, Poesie e racconti, op.cit., p. 43.

21 In *I Malavoglia*, Verga introduces the photograph in order to convey the real and actual, which speaks louder than the words. The young Antonio Malavoglia who cannot write provides a self reproduction, in place of verbal communication. Boito uses the image in a far less obvious manner, which highlights the convergence of light and shade.

22 R. Quadrelli, *Arrigo Boito, Poesie e racconti*, op.cit., p. 57.

23 Ibid.

24 It would appear that in this poem, Boito is rejecting revolution and innovation, and the materialistic greed which encouraged speculation in the construction industry. To prove his point he provides images of domesticity relating to mythology (the ancient household gods), nature (with reference to the birds nesting in the gutters) and family ties (the shades of the dead flee as the old buildings give way to the new).

25 R. Quadrelli, *A. Boito, Poesie e racconti*, op.cit., p. 46.

26 Ibid., p. 47.

27 Ibid.

28 See D. Del Principe, *Rebellion, Death and Aesthetics in Italy. The Demons of Scapigliatura*, Associated University Presses, New York, London, Ontario, 1966, p. 166.

29 Boito provides a further degree of complexity re: the 'mummy' and the 'torso' with regard to gender. The term 'mummia' is feminine, which allows the reader consider the form as feminine, 'torso' is masculine, but it belongs in this case to Venus. Such fusions and confusion contributes to the duality applied in both poems.

30 R. Quadrelli, *Arrigo Boito, Poesie e racconti*, op.cit., p. 48.

31 A smiliar vocabulary, to indicate Eastern exoticism is used in the libretto *Otello*, I, iii: 'Poi mi guidavi ai fulgidi deserti/all'arse arene, al tuo materno suol'.

32 R. Quadrelli, *Arrigo Boito, Poesie e racconti*, op.cit., p. 49.

33 Ibid., pp. 49-50.

34 Ibid., p. 51

35 Ibid.

36 Ibid., p. 55.

37 Ibid., p. 52. Adelaide Sozzi-Casanova, in her study *La Scapigliatura* op.cit., p. 16, reminds us that Boito, in the poems 'A una mummia' and 'Un torso', evokes past civilizations, i.e. the Egyptians and Greek.

38 Ibid., p. 53.

39 Ibid., p. 55.

40 Ibid., p. 56.

41 See D. Del Principe, *Rebellion, Death and Aesthetics in Italy*, op.cit., pp. 114-16.

42 R. Quadrelli, *Arrigo Boito, Poesie e racconti*, p. 70.

43 Ibid., p. 71.

44 Ibid.

45 Ibid. Illusions are seen to be as fleeting as poetic metre. Boito has emphasized a relationship between poetic form and ideal in 'Dualismo' and 'Case nuove'. Duality is expressed through variety and alternation of metre. A further irony is contained in 'Lezione d'anatomia' in so far as the stanzas in the poem contain six lines, and not four, as in the example of 'finzion fuggevole.' In *Re Orso* the use of polymetrical forms will demonstrate a more decisive move towards literary reform and the contrast and cohabitation of Art and Science.

46 Ibid., p. 72.

47 Ibid.

48 See V. Marini, *Arrigo Boito tra Scapigliatura e classicismo*, Loescher, Turin, 1968, pp. 1-2. Here we are reminded that Boito was the sole member of Scapigliatura who possessed the self confidence to rise above the basic antitheses of the other members of the group.

49 See M. Lavagetto, *Boito*, opere, op.cit., p. 43.

50 For an approach to the theoretic aspirations of the Milanese 'bohemians' see: F. Spera, *Il principio dell'antiletteratura: Dossi, Faldella, Imbriani*, Liguori, Naples, 1976.

51 The editions of A. Galetti, Milan, 1921 and P. Nardi, in *A. Boito, Tutti gli scritti*, op.cit., contain the 1902 version.

52 *Re Orso* was in fact presented as a puppetshow in Turin.

53 G. Scarsi, *Scapigliatura e Novecento*, op.cit., p. 195.

54 R. Quadrelli, *Arrigo Boito, Poesie e racconti*, op.cit., p. 19

55 B. Croce, *La letteratura della nuova Italia, saggi critici* (2nd ed.), Laterza, Bari, 1921, pp. 257-74.

56 R. De Rensis, *Lettere di A. Boito*, op.cit., pp. 169-70.

57 H. Busch (editor and translator), *Verdi's 'Otello' e 'Simon Boccanegra'*, I. Clarendon Press, Oxford, 1988, p. 793.

58 M. Lavagetto (editor), *Boito, opere*, op.cit., p. 45.

59 The pure and beautiful Oliba confronts the lascivious monster Orso. As a cross between Diana and Eve she presents the apple, poisoned at the core. One also notes the prevalance of a poisoned apple in legends and fairy-tales.

60 In her study *La Scapigliatura*, op.cit., p. 120, Adelaide Sozzi-Casanova claims that the central theme of the work is that of remorse, which accompanies man in life and after death.

61 As a reflection of the 'Mal de Siècle' *Re Orso* contains a certain affinity to the writing of the *Cannibili* of today. One must also bear in mind that at this period in his life, Boito had rejected the musical style of Verdi.

62 See Chapter I.

63 M. Lavagetto, *Boito,opere*, op.cit., p. 50. See Leopardi Canti, Rizzoli, Milan, pp. 94-95. One recalls that in the libretto *La Gioconda* (1876), after Victor Hugo's *Angelo, Tyran de Padoue* (1835), the blind mother La cieca is introduced, with the symbolic role of eerily seeing with blind eyes. Such a character does not exist in Hugo's drama.

64 Ibid., p. 52. Note also that 'canto fermo' is a medieval musical term.

65 The source of the voice at this point is not clear. It has qualities of the wind and a creature of the sea. In this respect the entire passage resembles the presentation of the 'banshee' in Irish Folklore: a woman, with the voice akin to the wind and a howling dog, who announces an imminent death.

66 M. Lavagetto (editor) *A. Boito*, Opere, op.cit., p. 80.

67 Ibid., p. 83-4.

68 Ibid., p. 84.

69 Ibid., p. 87.

70 A. Manzoni, *I promessi sposi*, XVI

71 M. Lavagetto (editor). *Boito, Opere*, op.cit., p. 90.

CHAPTER 3

Black Angel, White Devil.
Destruction, Disintegration and Reconciliation

Arrigo Boito's analytical technique in *Il libro dei versi – Re Orso* is directed towards the destruction and recreation of form, by means of a dismantling and reassembly of constituent parts of the poetic whole. This is clearly seen to be the case in 'A una mummia', 'Un torso' and 'Lezione d'anatomia'. The effects vary from the grotesque to the pathetic, and the scientific monitoring of the creative process provides the high point of Boito's 'duality' or 'dualismo'. In *Re Orso* however, the art is considerably more impure as the perception of the work and its interpretation is based, not on the analysis of single figures or episodes, but rather on the combination and juxtaposition of separate forms i.e. Orso/Oliba, Orso/the worm, Oliba's head/the troubadour, Papiol/Trol. Since for Boito, Good is static and Evil active, and *Re Orso* is a work about Evil, the sense of purpose in variously timed movements, ranging from the violent to the continual and consistent, is particularly significant. The metrical forms corresponding to such movements, in turn create harmonic effect, pointing toward a totally new form of expression, where the affinity between words and music will be explored. In *Re Orso* Boito is on the way to becoming the writer and composer of *Mefistofele*, to one dramatically exploring philosophical progressions, contained in a musical form.

Re Orso is not regarded by critics as a philosophical work.[1] Rather, as in a game of lotto, the various numbers/characters, in diverse sequences, lead to a variety of conclusions. The forms, physical rather than abstract, conform to the 'morta poesia' of Dante's *Inferno*.[2] Orso, brutal, violent and mindless, is characterized by the poet, rather than intellectualized. *Mefistofele*, conceived at the time of his Parisian sojourn, in both its versions, represents a philosophy of Evil. The Devil Philosopher, is not a parody of Good but rather he parodies God. In the space between the writing of *Re Orso* and the final elaboration of *Mefistofele* (1868),

Boito has provided an entirely new view of the order of thought. He has redrawn the conventional image of the universe, to create a space dominated by the Superman or Evil Deity, who dwarfs the God of the Earth, over whom he towers.

In his reformed vision of the melodrama, Boito sets himself a gigantic, unbounded scale with Faust symbolizing Everyman, in a universe dissolving into intellectual abstractions. What was intended however, to inaugurate a new era in the history of artistic expression, resulted in one of the most spectacular failures in the history of the theatre. There were many contributing factors for its disastrous reception at its first performance at La Scala, Milan (1868). Apart from Boito's youthful arrogance, his open criticism of Verdi, and his negative approach to all artistic endeavours excepting his own, the real problem with the original *Mefistofele* was its length. When Boito decided to refashion the work, he destroyed all traces of the original music, except for two pieces which were published separately . The entire libretto of the original remains, and many portions of it were incorporated into the final version with little or no revision.[3] All critics who heard both versions agree that the duet 'Lontano, lontano, lontano' (Far, far away), Margherita's 'Spunta l'aurora pallida' (The pale dawn emerges) and the fugue which concludes Act II, exist in the 1875 version only. Luigi Baldacci calls it 'a complete work, in which poetry, music and the arts converge to express a single purpose; to this may be added also metaphysical philosophy and political philosophy.[4] The latter is particularly the case in the first version, in the Imperial Palace scene, and in the Battle Intermezzo. In negating Verdi's work and structural innovation, Boito literally discarded all previous forms. Yet the work is not stylistically of great significance. His dispensing with the aria as the centre of operatic activity and his over-use of the chorus, devoid of the heroic trapping of Verdi's later work (*Don Carlo* and *Aïda*) is in no way influential. Realistic opera in the hands of Mascagni, Catalani, Puccini, Cilea and Giordano developed in a totally different direction. It is therefore Boito the librettist and poet who moulded the new literary ideology.

The libretto of *Mefistofele* falls into a Prologue, four Acts and an Epilogue. In it the battle between light and shade is accorded philosophical exposition by means of dramatic illustrations from the real and ideal worlds. The devil philosopher Mefistofele, in reality the personification of the mind of mankind, in its absolute form, illustrates the human propensity towards Evil, which is justified, not in the form of scientific experiment, but in terms of rational exposition. This latter element marks Boito's intellectual advancement towards a reassessment and updating of enlightenment theory. This will be seen to its full advantage and expression dramatically in *Otello*, and in prose in the short story *L'alfier nero* (1867).[5]

Mefistofele represents not only a return to Reason, but also the redefinition of human reason and its inability to soar to the absolute heights of intellectual prowess. The God of man, in addition to the mind of man is dwarfed and parodied. The world itself is presented as a tiny glass ball which emits *crystalline* images of beauty.

Mefistofele: Il Dio piccin della piccina terra

                  Ognor traligna ed erra

                  E, al par di grillo saltellante, a caso

                  Spinge fra gli astri il naso.

                  Poi con tenace fatuità superba

                  Fa il suo trillo nell'erba.

                  Boriosa polve, tracotato; atòmo!

                  Fantasima dell'uomo!

                  E tale il fa quell'ebra illusione

                  Ch'egli chiama Ragione.[6]

                                Mefistofele, Prologue

                  (The tiny God of the tiny earth

                  loses his direction

                  continually, and gets lost.

                  And like a jumping cricket

                  indeterminately pushes his nose through the stars.

                  Then with unyielding proud conceit,

                  He chirps in the grass.

                  Arrogant dust, haughty atom!

                  Spectre of man. And that intoxicated illusion

                  Which he calls Reason renders him so.)

Boito's irony is in the tradition of Leopardi who by operating a miniature scale reduces man and his world to ridicule, in 'La ginestra'.[7] While Leopardi blames Nature, Boito parodies the 'small god of a small world', so magnifying evil and its Super-human symbol *Mefistofele*.

63

Faust is declared

> Il più bizzarro pazzo
> Ch'io mi conosca.[8]
>
> *Mefistofele*, Prologue
>
> (The most crazy madman,
> That I know)

In comparative terms, Faust's philosophy according to the Devil, is madness, while that of Mefistofele – Knowledge, is the ultimate ideal. The two protagonists indulge in a philosophical exchange:

Faust:	Come ti chiami?
Mefistofele:	La domanda è inezia
	Puërile per tal che gli argomenti
	Sdegna del Verbo e crede solo agli Enti
Faust:	In voi, messeri, il nome ha tal virtù
	Che rivela l'Essenza. Dimmi or su
	Chi sei tu dunque?
Mefistofele:	Una parte vivente
	Di quella forza che perpetuamente
	Pensa il Male e fa il Bene.
	Voglio il Nulla e del Creato
	La ruina universal
	É atmosfera mia vital
	Ciò che chiamasi peccato
	Morte e mal.[9]

> *Mefistofele*, Act I, 2.

Faust:	(What is your name?
Mefistofele:	That is a childishly inane question,
	for one who distains the arguments of the word
	and believes only in Being.
Faust:	In your case Sir, the name contains such
	virtue as to reveal the Essence. Tell me
	anyway who you are.

Mefistofele:	A living part of that force that
	perpetually thinks Evil and does Good...I desire
	Nothingness, and the universal ruin of Creation.
	The atmosphere essential to me
	is that which is called Sin, Death and Evil.)

Faust's question indicates a desire to comprehend new Beings, although he would disdain the Word, or the expressive, in order to penetrate scientifically to the Essence of things. Faust's words indicate speculation, whilst *Mefistofele* emerges as a nihilist, set to destroy creation and creativity. This argument will be developed on a social level in *Otello*, when Jago, as a human expression of Mefistofele will destroy the creativity and spontaneity of Otello. The contradictory element within the Faust/Mefistofele discourse, shows the devil thinking Evil and claiming to do Good. The essential conflict between the thought and its expression indicates the disintegration of the behavioural process accepted hitherto, and with it the destruction of man. It can also be interpreted as the reversal of the theological concept which accepts man as essentially good, yet born to sin.[10] This is Boito's most likely intention, since Evil personified (Mefistofele) defines Faust as 'il più bizzarro pazzo' in his search for an ideal as humanly perceived. The introduction of the term 'pazzo' (mad) is also significant, as it points to Boito's introduction of Reason, not merely in philosophical terms, but also as regards the psychological perception of behaviour. Reason and the rational are no longer merely applied to Science, but also to Nature and Life. Sanity is recognized. Its opposite, insanity or madness is dramatized.

The second Act brings Faust into contact with the actual realization of his dreams: the rustic maiden Margherita emerges as the image of perfection in miniature. She is converted however by Faust to the expression of superhuman voluptousness.

Faust:	Dalle labbra imporporate
	Spandi accento sovruman
	Parla, parla.[11]
	Mefistofele, Act II, I.

Faust:	(From your reddened lips, you outpour

Superhuman words,
Speak, speak.)

The rustic maiden has become a torrid seductress. Her psyche however, unable to withstand such a transformation of being and perception, collapses and she becomes insane: the pursuit of Science beyond human capacity causes madness. Reason, pushed to its limits, gives way to its opposite. Boito has already set out on the road towards the Pirandellian preoccupation with the loss of reason. When Margherita eventually recovers her sanity, her language comes to resemble mere dramatic declamation, devoid of lyrical innuendoes, and reminiscent of the chilling realism of Scapigliatura. In other words, the illusion is contained in the lyrical poetic expression ('Lezione d'anatomia'). Reality is stark and devoid of embellishment. Margherita consists then of a fusion of illusion and reality, the romantic and realistic. In her insane ravings there is contained a beauty and simplicity of expression which belie her situation.

> L'aura è fredda, il carcer fosco
> E la mesta anima mia·
> Come il passero del bosco
> Vola via.[12]
> > *Mefistofele*, Act III, I

> (The air is cold, the prison dark,
> And my sad soul flies away like the
> Sparrow in the wood.)

On recovering her sanity, Margherita's thoughts turn to death and burial:

> Vien, vo' narrarti il tetro ordin di tombe
> Che doman scaverai...là fra le zolle
> Più verdeggianti...stenderai mia madre
> Nel più bel sito del cimiter...discosto
> Ma pur vicino...scaverai la mia...[13]
> > *Mefistofele*, Act III, I.

(Come I wish to relate to you

the dismal series of graves that you will dig

tomorrow.

There amongst the greenest sods you will lay

my mother.

In the most beautiful location of the cemetery

You will dig mine...)

Margherita is the symbol of transience in life, as opposed to the absolute ideal represented by Elena (Helen of Troy). The latter is 'Forma ideal, purissima–della bellezza eterna!' (Ideal, most pure form of eternal beauty). Her impermanence is not the result of any shortcomings in her own being, but as a result of the human mind's inability to permanently focus on a perfect image. The dissolution or disintegration of the image is thus the result of human failing, in the face of the superhuman. The conflict is between mind and body, between the philosophical thought and the physical brain which contains it. The conclusion of the work finds Faust in search of the unattainable. This philosophic treatise on Art, scientifically and intellectually conceived, at its conclusion can be reduced to the following equation: for Faust, illusion proves to be reality which is rejected by the mind in favour of the attainable, but non-retainable, absolute illusion.

Boito has not merely presented a philosophical dramatization of the scientific analysis of Art, he has allied it to moral philosophy and the consequences of persistent pressures on the human psyche. The role of Mefistofele illustrates the presence and necessity of evil, and in the latter statement Boito is following the theological ruling of Saint Thomas Aquinas. In the case of rational beings, where freewill exists, every created rational being is capable of doing morally evil actions. Mefistofele states that human reason is an illusion: quell'ebra/illusione/Ch'egli chiama Ragion.[14] The Thomist teaching states however, that no rational creature is capable of reaching its final end by its own powers. The Devil fails however, to win Faust's soul, and if he indeed does win the argument, it is because Faust's earlier sequence of creative thoughts lacks permanence. Faust remains in search of an ideal, but the means by which it can be rationally and scientifically achieved remains a mystery. While Evil destroys and derides human faith, it cannot provide a substitute for it.

As early as 1851, Francesco Maria Piave in *Rigoletto* touched on the area of the psychological and self-analytical. Boito, in *Il libro dei versi* with the exception of the manifesto 'Dualismo', avoided the concept of the self: The subject is introduced in *Re Orso*, through the King's inability to expel the voices from his head. Had he so wished Boito could have developed the idea and produced the themes of Reason and insanity as dominant forces. However, in a legend, separated in time and subject from his readers' experience, he avoided the issue. *Mefistofele* is thus significant, not only on account of its linguistic approximation to musical expression, its departure from formulae in favour of creating a new form, but also for the introduction of loss of reason, resulting in madness. In a manner totally diverse from such Romantic writers as Grossi,[15] Cammarano, Pepoli and Romani, Boito in *Mefistofele* provides the spontaneous expression of insanity, alongside philosophical and scientific expositions. The result is an intellectual drama which may take its place in the history of psychologically oriented literary expression. In idealogical terms, Boito has now prepared the way for his adaptation of Shakespeare's *Otello* for Giuseppe Verdi.

Before proceeding to an analysis of Boito's adaptation of Shakespeare, some attention must be given to an important prose piece which closely follows the poetic works and preceeds by one year the first version of *Mefistofele*: *L'alfièr nero* (*The Black Bishop*). This is a short story first published in the *Politecnico*, March 1867. In it are revealed two new idealogical elements: the contrasting forces of light and darkness reduced to moves on a chess board and symbolized by the pieces. These are scientifically manipulated by the players, who are also drawn in striking contrast: one is a white American, the other is a negro. The game proceeds on two levels: the literal, which marks the progress on the chess board, and the psychological, which demonstrates the antithesis between Reason and emotion. The social dimension is also fundamental, as racism rears its ugly head. The tale concludes with Boito's use of the unexpected. A further innovation is however provided. The white man, unable to accept defeat by a negro, resorts to murder. But the power of the mind results in the insanity of the killer, whose sense of guilt and remorse is too great for his psyche to bear. The final explosion of 'dualismo' is contained in the fact that the mental pressure involved in a concentration between the forces of Reason and emotion, causes Reason, the victor, to ultimately break down and give way not merely to emotional expression, but to madness. Boito's duality is here at its most sophisticated. It is a prelude to Pirandellian thought, as shall be discussed in relation to *Il berretto a sonagli*. The basic ingredients of *Otello* are already present: a battle at sea preceding one of wits, a white Venetian and a black Moor, an act of violence leading to madness. However while the white rationalist of *L'alfier nero* brings about his own insanity, in *Otello* the emotional Moor, kills, not his opponent, but his most precious possession, and in sorrow and remorse turns his sword on himself. Both characters, as exercises in logic, contain their own justification.

A further feature of Boito's development begs consolidation: the emergence of 'duality' at all stages in his career, under diverse guises. In *Il libro dei versi*, it is sophisticated and complex, intellectualizing parody, while avoiding dramatization. In *Re Orso* to use Boito's own term, it is at its most 'strambo' (crazy). In *Mefistofele*, the duality of idealogical processes directed towards Evil is personified. With the abstraction taking physical form, parody of good in the form of Mefistofele is achieved. *L'alfier nero* and *Otello* take the psychological process a step further: Boito presents the raw world of raw passion and shows how they contain their own rationale. From the mind of the poet/philosopher/librettist, there emerge several devils: from the brute Re Orso, to the intellectual Mefistofele, from the American racist to the mind of the military man set on revenge. The stage is now set for the enactment of a scientific experiment based on psychological prowess, in the libretto *Otello*.

The plot of Shakespeare's *Othello* derives from Giraldi Cinthio's seventh *novella*, in the third decade of his *Hecartommihi* (Venice 1566). Boito's most important primary source was F. Victor Hugo's French translation of Shakespeare of which Boito possessed at least three copies.[16] Although Boito carried out extensive work on the text in 1879, after his reconciliation with the composer, Verdi does not appear to have committed himself totally to the venture until he had the opportunity of working closely with Boito. This came about in 1880, when Verdi wrote to his future librettist from Genoa, asking him to provide some revisions to the libretto of *Simon Boccanegra* (1857). The most substantial additions provided by Boito are the Grand Council, scene of Act I, and Paolo's monologue, Act II.2. He also rewrote in full the first two scenes of the third act.[17] Boito's *Otello* is a concentrated, condensed and simplified account of Shakespeare's *Othello*.[18] In telling the tale of the Moor of Venice, the Italian librettist reflects the essential elements of the English tragedian's plot. He refines the action, dispensing with unnecessary scenes and characters, until a psychologically changed presentation of human reactions is attained. By eliminating Act I of Shakespeare's tragedy, he provides unity of place, allowing the entire action to evolve in Cyprus.[19] He deprives the drama of some degree of its racist nature by dispensing with Desdemona's father.[20] This allows Otello and Desdemona to exist on equal footing, from a dramatic viewpoint. It alters the Shakespearean dimension of the drama as a conflict between two civilizations. Instead Boito's text emerges as a juxtaposition of good and evil. The conflict between 'black' and 'white' is no longer essentially between husband and wife, but rather between two men: the white devil, the Venetian Jago and the black angel, the Moor Otello. This also somewhat robs the action of romantic interest. Desdemona, as uncorruptible good, is merely a pawn in a Machiavellian game, in which Boito, further developing his doctrine of the relationships between the forces of light and darkness, demonstrates how good may be utilized as the means by which evil is achieved. Moreover, the basic conflict between a white devil and a black angel assumes an Elizabethan quality in the work. In addition to communicating lust, heroism and violence, the world of Webster's *The Duchess of Malfi* and *The White Devil* is conjured up. This succeeds in preserving the spirit of the early seventeenth-century. *Otello* then like the majority of Boito's earlier works incorporates duality. It carries to a new level of subtlety the philosophy of Art and Life expounded in the poems of *Il libro dei versi*.[21] Boito, having established the heroic context of events, shifts the emphasis of the main action, to provide a theoretic exposition of the Science of behaviour. The drama evolves as a dramatized exposition of the effect of the analytical on the spontaneous. Jago the rational analyst, subjects the emotional expressionism of Otello to a scientific experiment. He commands the consciousness of Otello in pursuit of destruction. Intellectual evil possesses the mind of good. The white devil manipulates a black angel, albeit a fallen one. Boito's greatest achievement is that of not merely having updated the enlightenment battle between Reason and Emotion, but of having carried it to a new degree of originality. He carries it far beyond a juxtaposition of Art and Science, but rather applies psychological reality to the rules of logic and objectivity, in order to pave the way for the theatre of the absurd, with its probings of motivation, culminating in the contrasting forces of Reason and Madness.

In the libretto *Otello* the battle between good and evil is initially projected in terms of the armed struggle between the Christian Venetian State and forces of the infidel Moslem. As Otello returns home he must battle with the forces of nature. He is symbolic of the artist, the 'istrion' of 'Dualismo' who walks a tightrope between virtue and vice. Tossed towards the heavens and the bottom of the sea he is powerless in the hands of destiny. Yet as a heroic giant he, in his Venetian ship fills the space between the forces of Nature and infinity and is revealed and obscured by the natural forces of light and darkness:

Montano:	Or s'affonda
	Or s'inciela...
Metà del coro:	Nelle nubi si cela e nel mar
	E alla luce dei lampi ne appar.[22]

Otello, Act I.1

Montano:	(Now it sinks
	Now it rises towards the sky
Half Chorus:	It is concealed in the clouds and the sea
	And appears with the flashes of lightening.)

Boito employs several degrees of perception from the opening of his text, in order to straightaway present visual impressions of clear-cut objects, accompanied by heroic sound:

Alcuni:	uno squillo!
Altri:	uno squillo!
Tutti:	Ha tuonato il cannon![23]

Otello, Act I.1

Some:	(A blast!
Others:	A blast!
All:	The cannon has sounded.)

Boito continues the visual effect as the ship is perceived hitting the rocks. Dinghies are thrown and finally the heroic giant emerges. The victory of Otello the warrior is highlighted, in preparation for the defeat of Otello the man. The conflict between good and evil has already been initiated. Throughout the work the voice of goodness is expressed in a series of prayers. In Act I, the chorus in a collective prayer, implores God to allow the safe return of Otello. It cries out:

> Dio fulgor della bufera!
> Dio sorriso della duna!
> Salva l'arca e la bandiera
> Della veneta fortuna!

Tu che reggi gli astri e il Fato!
Tu che imperi al mondo e al ciel!
Fa che in fondo al mar placato
Posi l'ancora fedel.[24]

Otello, Act I.1

(Oh God, splendour of the blizzard,
Oh God, smile of the sands!
Save the ship and the flag of Venetian fortune.
You who control the stars and fate!
You who reign over the world and the heavens
Allow that the loyal anchor rest in the
depths of a calm sea.)

The second prayer, one of thanksgiving, establishes Otello as a Christian leader. His entry has no equivalent in Shakespeare:

Esultate! L'orgoglio musulmano
Sepolto è nel mar, nostro e del ciel è
Gloria!
Dopo l'armi lo vinse uragano.[25]

Otello, Act I, 1

(Rejoice! The Moslem pride is buried in
the sea. Ours and heavens is the glory
After the armed victory, the storm is
laid low.)

The single moment of tenderness before Jago's poison begins to act, is contained in the love duet. It highlights Otello's qualities as warrior:

Desdemona: Mio superbo guerriero!
               Quanti tormenti,
               Quanti mesti sospiri e quanta speme
               Ci condusse ai soavi abbracciamenti.[26]

Otello, Act III, 3.

Desdemona: (My proud warrior! What torment,
               How many sad sighs and what hope
               Lead us to such beauteous embraces.)

It provides a short insight into Otello's past:

Desdemona: Poi mi guidavi ai fulgidi deserti, All'arse arene,
               al tuo materno suol.[27]
                              Otello, Act I, 3.

Desdemona: (Then you brought me to the shining deserts
               To the burned sand-dunes
               to your homeland.)

The duet and the first Act of the tragedy concludes with the prayer that their love remain unchanged with the passing of time:

Desdemona: Disperda il ciel gli affanni
               E amor non muti col mutar degli anni.
Otello: A questa tua preghiera
               Amen risponda la celeste schiera
Desdemona: *Amen* risponda.[28]
                              Otello, Act I, 3.

Desdemona: (May heaven dispel suffering
               and may love not change with the changing
               years.
Otello: May the heavenly ranks respond *Amen* to
               your prayer.
Desdemona: *Amen*.)

Desdemona and Otello complement each other as opposing forces of good: one fair, the other dark, male and female, gentle and courageous. Desdemona repeats Otello's *Amen risponda* in order to support his ideal and to provide a harmonious echo within the melodies of the duet. Later Boito, in the case of Otello and Jago, will employ a similar technique of repetition, for a sinister purpose, as evil enters the mind of good. At this point in the drama, good echoes good for the last time, as Otello and Desdemona are physically and melodically one. The musical embrace is contained in the alternation of voices and repetition of Amen.

This echo within the duet, preparing for noctural tranquillity and silence, is in itself an echo of the impressionistic poetics of the chorus, preceding Iago's drinking song. 'Fuoco di gioia' (Fire of joy) occupies a key function in providing symbolic poetic imagery in a pre-Romantic vein. Identifiable with the passages in the early librettos of Verdi by Temistocle Solera and later work by Salvatore Cammarano,[29] the flame is identified with love that blazes, sparkles, flickers, grows dull and dies. It is a poetic prediction of the end of the love interest in the libretto, but also of the death of the style of poetry utilized in the early choruses in Act I, and identifiable with neo-classical Alfierian imagery. It points towards a new poetic medium and diverse linguistic device which will extinguish both spontaneity of expression on the part of Otello and the traditional symbolism adapted by Boito's predecessors Solera and Cammarano.

> Guizza, sfavilla, crepita, avvampa
> Fulgido incendio – che invade il cor
>
> Fuoco di gioia rapida brilla!
> Rapida passa fuoco d'amor!
> Splende, s'oscura, palpita, oscilla,
> L'ultimo guizzo, lampeggia e muor.[30]
>> *Otello*, Act I, 1.
>
> (It sparkles, crackles, blazes,
> Bright burning that invades the heart
>
> Fire of joy, gleams rapidly!
> Rapidly passes, fire of love!
> It blazes, it dims, it trembles, wavers,
> The final flicker, flashes and dies.)

In Act I of *Otello*, the prayers reflect hope, faith and love. The entire social and ethical vision is overturned in Act II. The Science of evil is expounded by one who believes in a God of cruelty who fashions his creatures to his image and likeness, that they may dissolve into nothingness. The Christian ethic is overturned by Iago, in a process of anihilation. Boito, treating of the essence and effect of evil, in psychological terms, allows Iago's prayer, his 'Credo', or rather anti-creed occupy the central position within the libretto. It carries the drama from the level of moral, to intellectual conflict. Evil declares its intentions as the psychological implications of doubt, uncertainty and suspicion are unfolded. Evil enters the mind of Otello, sows doubts, it becomes the echo of the Moor's thoughts. Repetition is effected in order to provoke further consideration. Boito expounds a Science of Evil, based on the Art of insinuation. As in 'Lezione d'anatomia' Science utilizes nature to provide positivist results: the critic analyses and dissects in order to find a hidden meaning. In Boito's *Otello*, Iago is indeed inspired by and symbolic of scientific progression. His victim is purity, spontaneity and innocence: Art in its contrasting and conflicting forms: the white woman and the black man.

In the Production Book for the Opera *Otello* compiled by Giulio Ricordi,[31] the character of Iago is presented as follows: 'Jago is Envy. Jago is a scoundrel. Jago is a critic.' Ricordi also insists that Boito's critic is in no way to be confused with Mefistofele. He is not a human demon, 'Jago's every word comes from the man, from the villainous man, but from the man. He must be young and handsome... Cinzio Giraldi,...calls Jago: 'un alfiero di bellissima presenza ma della più scellerata natura che mai fosse uomo del mondo."[32] (an ensign of most handsome appearance, but of the most evil nature possible on this earth). In other words Boito, having provided the personification of the philosophy of Evil in *Mefistofele*, now presents 'the thing itself' evil incarnate. It is my belief that Boito's literary and scientific symbolism is contained in an interpretation of the Shakespearian definition:

'I am nothing if not critical'[33]

Othello, Act II, 1.

Rather than be seen merely as critical, Boito and Ricordi consider him a critic: 'Io non sono che un critico.'[34] The character of Iago is thus developed to the point where his 'credo' becomes the central declamation of the work. The fundamental expression of the Christian faith has become a denial, a negation of a just God, and of the free will of man. Man in the form of Jago is predestined to be evil:[35]

> Credo in un Dio crudel che m'ha creato
> Simile a sè, e che nell'ira io nomo.
> Dalla viltà d'un germe o d'un atomo
> Vile son nato
> Sono scellerato
> Perchè son uomo
> E sento il fango originario in me
>
> ....
>
> ....
>
> Credo che il giusto è un istrïon beffardo
> E credo l'uom gioco d'iniqua sorte.[36]
> > *Otello*, Act II, 2.

> (I believe in a God of cruelty, who has created
> me in his image
> And that in anger I name.
> From the baseness of an embryo or of an atom.
> Base, I was born.
> I am a scoundrel because I am a man
> And I feel the mud of origin in me
>
> ....
>
> ....
>
> I believe that the just man is a clownish
> Performer,
> And I believe man to be a pawn
> Of iniquious fortune.)

Divine mercy and justice are converted to cynicism in a game of hazard. Man is the expression of a cruel Science, the 'homuculus' of the demented chemist of 'Dualismo'.[37] The just man, is the tightrope walker of the same poem,[38] who at this stage of Boito's rationalisation is regarded as a liar, in essence and appearance:

> E nel viso e nel cuor,

Che tutto è in lui bugiardo.[39]

Otello, Act II, 2.

(And in expression and in heart
(I believe) that all his attributes are lies.)[40]

In the same Act, in the following scene Desdemona, woman, is venerated as a religious object, a sacred image, adored by children and sailors, and compared to the Madonna:

Marinai: Vogliamo Desdemona
                Coi doni nostri
                Come un'immagine
                Sacra adornar.[41]

                (With our gifts
                We wish to adorn Desdemona
                As a sacred object.)

Desdemona is presented with lilies and necklaces of coral and pearls, representing the natural treasures of the sea.[42] The final formal prayer of the work, the 'Ave Maria' or 'Hail Mary', places Desdemona in absolute opposition to Jago. The 'Creed' and 'Hail Mary' represent the two basic prayers of the Christian Church. Yet while the woman prays with the traditional words of the prayer, Jago perverts, distorts and parodies the declaration of faith. From this, one may deduct that in poetic terms the two opposing characters are Jago and Desdemona. Sincerity and parody are juxtaposed. With the philosophical oppostion of Science and Art, Jago and Otello occupy centre stage.

Although Boito's source is Shakespeare, studied closely in the translation by F. Victor Hugo, the Italian poet's originality consists of a re-invention of linguistic forms, which carries Italian poetic diction from the more clearly defined contrasts and juxtapositions of 'dualismo' to a psychologically oriented dramatization of abstractions. Doubt, uncertainty, suspicion, unease, become the real protagonists of the work in the second Act, as they take control of the physical presence and movement of Otello. The drama develops as an exercise in manipulation: Jago directs

Otello's thoughts from without, whilst the latter suffers an intense internal struggle, resulting in his physical collapse. Stage direction assumes an explanatory function with almost the status of a third party, as controlled, diabolical logic containing its own rational provokes uncontrolled passion:

Otello:	Nol credi onesto?
Iago:	(imitando Otello) Onesto?
Otello:	(con innocenza) Che ascondi nel tuo cuore?
Iago:	Che ascondo in cor signore?
Otello:	"Che ascondo in cor signore?"

Pel cielo! Tu sei l'eco dei detti miei.[43]
Otello, Act II, 3.

Otello:	(Do you not believe him to be honest?
Iago:	(imitating Otello) Honest?
Otello:	(innocently) What are you hiding in your heart?
Iago:	Sir, what am I hiding in my heart?
Otello:	Sir, what are you hiding in your heart?

By heaven! You are the echo of my words.)

Boito's use of repetiton has a dual purpose. Iago repeats the words of Otello, in order to contemplate and, in a sense, to play for time. This also has the effect of analytical probing which creates doubt in the Moor's mind. As Otello then expresses his realization that Jago is the echo of his words, paradoxically Otello becomes the echo of Iago, as well as of himself. Boito is linguistically placing Iago's repetition between Otello's, questioning his opinion and his utlization of that opinion to form a new attitude of mind, goaded by jealousy and doubt. In other words Iago as evil, malice and jealousy has entered the mind of Otello, changing the disposition of the 'honest' Moor forever:

Iago:	Temete, signor, la gelosia

———————————————-

Otello:	Misera mia!!...No, il vano sospettar
	nulla giova.
	Pria del dubbio l'indagine, dopo il dubbio,

la prova.[44]

Otello, Act II, 3.

Iago: (Sir, beware of jealousy.
                 _____

Otello: Oh misfortune!!... No, vain suspicion is
                 Pointless.
                 Before doubt comes investigation, after doubt
                 comes the proof.)

As diabolical reason takes posession of Otello, he becomes the symbolic personification of logic and spontaneity[45], reason and emotion, all struggling for supremacy. The hopelessness of Otello's case is accentuated by the fact that reason in this
instance is the Science of psychological manipulation, effected by one answering
to a God of cruelty and evil, in whose likeness he has claimed to have been created. The 'duality' or 'dualismo' of Scapigliatura no longer merely consists of contrasts and confrontation leading to complexity. It has been carried to a new degree
of contradiction resulting in the overturning of logic, while at the same time pointing to the folly of such deductions. Boito has placed the semantic doubt before
investigation, (pria del dubbio l'indagine), while the ultimate sense implies investigation before doubt. But since one rarely conducts an investigation without cause,
it can be deducted that Otello has accepted doubt, while attempting to minimize its
effect. Jago's next lines contain 'honesty', 'suspicion' and 'fraud' which seldom
co-exist in the minds of the well disposed:[46]

Jago: Vigilate, sovente le oneste e ben create
                 coscienze, non sospettano la frode.[47]
                 Otello, Act II, 3.

                 Be vigilant, often honest and well formed
                 dispositions don't suspect fraud.

As Otello fears that such a horrific combination of abstractions should prove positive, he cries out for certainty, fact and proof:

Più orrendo di ogni orrenda ingiuria
Dell'ingiuria è il sospetto.

—————————————

La prova io voglio! Voglio
La certezza.[48]

Otello, Act II, 5.

(More horrible than every horrible affront
is suspicion of affront
I want proof. I want certainty.)

Once again Boito has organized the succession of events, scenes and words in order to display the destructive force at work. The effect of such a force is seen to be self destruction: although Otello fears certainty, he cries out for it. He has become Shakespeare's 'green eyed monster' which consumes itself:

O, beware jealousy;
It is the green-ey'd monster, which doth mock
That meat it feeds on.[49]

Otello, Act III, 3.

Jago: Temete, signor, la gelosia!
É un'idra fosca, livida, cieca, col suo veleno
Sè stessa attosca...[50]

Otello, Act II, 3.

(Beware of Jealousy Sir,
It is a dark hydra, black and blind,
With its poison, itself it poisons.)

Otello at this point has evolved as a psychological drama in which the physical and abstract are complemented by the spontaneous and intellectual. The romantic realism of Piave is now carried towards psychological immediacy as the stage becomes both the source of representation of life and a laboratory in which the 'chimico demente'[51] not only effects movement and behaviour but also psychological progressions. Caught in a spider's web of subtle insinuation, the gigantic black fly,

Otello has become a monster, created by the psychiatrist who has brought about the mental collapse of his victim. With the victory of Science, Otello has been programmed to complete the physical destruction of Beauty and Innocence. Yet his sources of justification are not only false and unjust, but also border on the absurd. They are both intangible and tangible: Cassio's dream and the hankerchief. Within the mind of Otello they create a battle between the forces of darkness and light. Not surprisingly they imply darkness (era la notte...It was night) and light (più bianco...che fiocco di neve...Whiter than a snowflake). As symbolic of the subconscious, and the conscious attention to refined detail, they join forces in the undoing of Otello.

Cassio's dream is confirmed in an atmosphere of mystery, insinuatingly effective, enunciated in onomatopoeiac tones, leading to the crucial 'Il rio destin impreco che al Moro ti donò' (I curse the cruel fate that gave thee to the Moor). Here Boito's text closely resembles its source. However, the Italian poet focuses on the word 'dream' in a manner which accentuates the implication of reality. In Shakespeare one reads:

Othello:	O monstrous, monstrous.
Iago:	Nay, this was but his dream
Othello:	But this denoted a foregone conclusion.
Iago:	Tis a shrewd doubt, though it be but a dream
	And this may help to thicken other proofs.[52]

Othello, Act III, 3.

Boito provides:

Otello:	Oh! Che mostrousa colpa!
Jago:	Io non narrai
	Che un sogno
Otello:	Un sogno che rivela un fatto.
Jago:	Un sogno che può dar forma di prova
	ad altro indizio.[53]

Otello, Act II, 5.

Otello:	(Oh what monstrous guilt!
Jago:	I merely told of a dream.

| Otello: | A dream that reveals a fact. |
| Jago: | A dream that can give substance to further evidence.) |

For the second time, Otello and Jago echo each other's pronouncement of 'sogno' (dream). The transformation of doubt to certainty and of shadow to substance is effected as 'sogno' (dream) by implication becomes 'fatto' (fact), based on 'forma di prova' (form of proof). This leads to the introduction of the handkerchief: a love token, artistically woven, white as snow, but with a sinister purpose. Jago refers to it as 'una ragna', meaning a trap, a snare or threadbare piece of material. The term 'ragnatela' means spider's web. As a web, it imprisons Otello. It represents the antithesis of the Moor: it is small, he is great; it is white, he is black; it appears wondrous, but it has a hidden agenda. At this point Boito is, through the image of the handkerchief, weaving together aspects of his technique already apparent in *Re Orso*, with the psychological and scientific dimensions already established in Act II of *Otello*. The grotesque and brutal world of *Re Orso* is refined, yet magnified in scale. If one focuses on Boito's methodology, a journey towards the absurd becomes apparent. The Moor's psychological struggle with himself is portrayed on a vast scale. It is seen from without and within. The mind of the hero is the true subject of the central section of the drama. Nonetheless the figure of Otello is turned around: he is trapped by a tiny object, whose symbolic function is to reduce the lion of Venice to a fly caught in a web of intrigue. Overcome by mental anguish, his mind is incapable of rejecting the image of Desdemona clasped in the arms of Cassio, and he is unable to refrain from uttering the word which has become an obsession:

il fazzoletto.[54]

Otello, Act III, 9.

(The handkerchief.)

As the internal struggle results in a loss of consciousness, Jago cries out:

Ecco il Leone!...[55]

(Behold the Lion!)

The lion has been reduced to a senseless object. Boito has succeeded in providing a game of alternation with regard to scale. His 'dualismo' does not merely allow for duplicity of purpose, but for the transformation of the object of analysis from a source of dignity, to one of ridicule. The direct cause of such a metamorphosis is a mere handkerchief:

> Più bianco, più lieve
> Che fiocco di neve,
> Che nube tessuta
> Dall'aure del ciel.[56]
>
> *Otello*, Act III, 5.

> (Whiter, lighter
> Than a snowflake,
> Than a cloud woven,
> By the breeze of heaven.)

Both parody and absurdity are here effected. The hero has been degraded and destroyed. His reconstruction will later serve towards the physical destruction of Desdemona and himself.

Although the scientific experiment has seen evil to conquer, the poetic image of death incorporates beauty in the face of misfortune. Unlike youth, poetry and beauty as projected in 'Lezione d'anatomia', Desdemona retains the innocence and purity that her death serves to reinforce. The death of the lovers re-establishes both poetry and truth. It would appear that Boito has here intended his 'dualismo' to come full circle. In addition to complexity of character, juxtaposition of attributes and the scientific exposition of the process of transformation and destruction, the poet both musically and linguistically returns to a purity of concept, as is illustrated in the final act. It has already been noted that the Christian creed enunciated by Jago in Act II, is perverted and parodied, occupying the focal in the libretto. As Jago's opposite, Desdemona in Act IV prays, using the traditional form of the 'Hail Mary', with few variations. Although about to die, Desdemona re-establishes the purity of poetry and prayer in a fusion of the profane (in the 'Willow Song') and the sacred (in the 'Hail Mary'). Boito is thus providing reconciliation of attributes with the addition of an individual supplication from a representative of those wronged in life:

> Prega per chi sotto l'oltraggio piega
> La fronte e sotto la malvagia sorte;[57]
>> *Otello*, Act IV, 2.

> (Pray for those who bow their heads
> To insult and cruel destiny.)

Truth is finally established when Jago refuses to deny his crimes as he flees from his accusers:

Otello (a Jago):   Ah! Discolpati!!
Jago (fuggendo): No.[58]
>> *Otello*, Act IV, 4.

Otello (to Jago): Ah, justify yourself!
Jago (fleeing):   No.

Humility and heroic grandeur is combined in the dramatization of the death of Otello:

> Ecco la fine
> Del mio cammin...O Gloria! Otello fu.[59]

> (Behold the end of my path...O glory. Othello was.)

As in the case of Gioconda[60] Boito has traced a path, symbolic of human progression, illuminated by Beauty and Art and crossed by folly and depravity. Desdemona's murder and Jago's discovery do not merely restore beauty but also piety and the veneration of the sacred. The prayer at the conclusion of Act I is re-evoked: the kiss motif is repeated, following the poetic recomposition of the dead figure already assumed into heaven:

> E tu, come sei pallida!
> E stanca e muta, e bella,

84

Pia creatura nata sotto maligna stella
Fredda come la casta tua vita, e in cielo
assorta.[61]

(And you, how pale you are! And wan
and silent and beautiful. A pious creature,
born under an evil star. Cold, as your
chaste life, and risen to heaven.)

As the final conflict between Good and Evil is resolved, order is re-established. Desdemona's piety and chastity are confirmed. Jago's satanic strategy (l'arti nefande) is uncovered and Otello's past glory is confirmed but declared finished. Physical and thematic unity is restored as the dying Otello embraces the dead figure, to the verbal and musical expression of love:

Un bacio...un bacio ancora...un altro
bacio.[62]

(A kiss, another kiss, yet another kiss.)

The poets of Scapigliatura have been credited with the rediscovery of evil and with having provided literature with its first ventures into Modernism. It can also be argued that the basic artistic dictates of creativity and destruction have been refashioned and re-evaluated by Arrigo Boito. In the *Libro dei versi*, Boito decomposes and reconstructs the symbolic object, in order to allow for the identification of various art forms. In *Re Orso* decapitation highlights the intellectual dimension which the poet chooses to ignore in the course of the poem, and consolidates the use of parody of brute force. *Mefistofele* is a dramatization of the abandonment of the traditional dramatic and musical form, which contains a disintegration of the ideal. The latter occurs, as has already been noted, because of human inability to permanently focus on and maintain an ideal image, projected by the imagination. Art cannot thus be perfected, since its creation and consistency remains a mystery and its existence is the result of the harmonization of mind and body. In *Otello* Boito arrives at the destruction and reconciliation of natural forms as a result of scientific programming. However, while Art and ideal in *Mefistofele* are seen to lack permanence, so Science in *Otello* is seen to triumph in terms of the result of the experiment. On its completion, the subjects regain their original attributes. Truth and facts dominate as Jago's evil is revealed, and Desdemona's innocence realized. Otello, if only to die, reassumes his heroic dignity. Destruction has here given way to reconciliation, as the stage/laboratory is cleared. Only the equipment has been consumed in the positivist exposition of facts. Yet the experiment contains its own tragedy: intrinsic critical analysis has destroyed both black and white. Reconciliation is effected in death:

La morte è il nulla.

(Death is nothingness.)

Jago's dogma is denied as Otello confirms that Desdemona has been taken to heaven. Evil has conquered on the battlefield and in the laboratory, but the moral order prevails.

NOTES

1   See M. Lavagetto, *Boito, Opere*, op.cit., p. XX
2   See Dante, *Purgatorio*, I, I.7: 'Qui la morta poesíe resuga'.
3   For an analysis of both versions of *Mefistofele* see G. Scarsi, 'Rapporto poesia –musica' in *Arrigo Boito*, op.cit., pp. 44-62; For a synopsis of the principal differences between the two versions see J. Nicolaisen, *Italian Opera in Transition 1871-1893*, UMI Press, Michigan, 1980, pp. 128-34.
4   L. Baldacci, *La musica in Italiano: libretti d'opera dell'Ottocento*, Rizzoli, Milan, 1997, p. 247.
5   See R. Quadrelli *Arrigo Boito. Poesie e racconti*, op.cit., pp. 153-70.
6   See, A. Boito, *Mefistofele*, Ricordi, Milan, 1979, pp. 7-8.
7   See G. Leopardi, *Canti*, Rizzoli, Milan, 1974, 'La ginestra', l. 202-12, 231-6, pp. 183-4. Leopardi also upbraids man for having abandoned the enlightened path of reason, at l. 53-8, p. 179. A miniature scale is also adopted in 'Dialogo di un folletto e uno gnomo,' *Operette morali*, Rizzoli, Milan, 1976, pp. 100-5.
8   A. Boito, *Mefistofele*, op.cit., p. 8.
9   Ibid., p. 19-20.
10 For a philosophical elucidation of the existence and necessity of evil see: C. Connellan, *Why Does Evil Exist?* Exposition Press, Hicksville, New York, 1974.
11 A.Boito, *Mefistofele*, op.cit., p. 23.
12 Ibid., p. 33.
13 Ibid., p. 35.
14 A. Boito, *Mefistofele*, op.cit., p. 8.
15 Tommaso Grossi's novel in verse Ildegonda (1820), contains what may be regarded as the first 'romantic mad scene'. See *Ildegonda*, part IV (conclusion). Also D. O'Grady 'Grossi, Manzoni e l'evoluzione della monaca', in *Manzoni/Grossi, II, Atti del XIV Congresso Nazionale di Studi Manzoniani*, Casa Manzoni, Milan, 1991; D. O'Grady, *The Last Troubadours, Poetic Drama in Italian Opera*, 'Of Realism and Delerium', op.cit., pp. 128-51.
16 A copy of *La tragédie d'Othello, Le Maure de Venise*, in *Oeuvres Complètes de W. Shakespeare*, vol 5 (1860), belonging to Boito is now in the 'Museo teatrale alla Scala'. It contains many notes, underlinings and comments, and is clearly the poet's principal working source. For an English translation of Cinthios work see H. Busch (editor) Verdi's 'Othello' and 'Simon Boccanegra' pp. 757-64. (See details below).
17 For considerations on the libretto of *Simon Boccanegra* see C. Dapino (editor) *Il teatro italiano*, V. Vol.2, Enaudi, Turin, 1984, pp. 177-81; D. Goldin, *La vera fenice*, Einaudi, Turin, 283-314; H. Busch (editor), *Verdi's 'Othello' and 'Simon Boccanegra'* (revised version), in Letters and Documents, Clarendon Press, Oxford, 1988.
18 For the sources of Shakespeare's *Othello* see: H. Busch (editor), *Verdi's 'Othello' and 'Simon Boccanegra'*, op.cit., pp. 756-64.
19 Boito used what he believed best from Act I and incorporated it in the 'love duet': E tu m'a-mavi per le mie sventure/Ed io t'amavo per la tua pietà, A. Boito, *Otello*, Ricordi, Milan, p. 22. (And you loved me on account of my misfortune/and I loved you on account of your pity. C.f. 'She loved me for the dangers I had pass'd/and I loved her that she did pity them' *Othello*, Act I, 3.
20 See Shakespeare's *Othello*, Act I,2: 'The sooty bosom/of such a thing as thou!' Ibid., Act I, 3. 'To fall in love with what she fear'd to look on?' Ibid., Act I,3. 'I am glad at soul I have no other child/For thy escape would teach me tyranny.'
21 This area is introduced in D. O'Grady, *The Last Troubadours*, op.cit., in the chapter 'Devil's advocate', pp. 180-201.
22 A. Boito, Otello, op.cit., p. 8.
23 Ibid.

24 Ibid., pp. 8-9.

25 Ibid., p. 10.

26 Ibid., p. 21.

27 Ibid., p. 22

28 Ibid, p. 23

29 The source of imagery of fire and flame in the pre-unification drama is Vittorio Alfieri (1749-1804). F.L. Arruga, *Incontri fra poeti*, Vita e pensiero, Milan, 1968, p. 240, has stressed the importance of Alfieri in the study of the operatic libretto. See S. Cammarano, *Il trovatore*, Act I, 2. 'Perigliosa fiamma' (perilous flame); Act II, l. 'Stride la vampa-sinistra splende – la tetra fiamma' (The flame shrieks, it blazes grimly – the dark flame); Act III, 6. 'Di quella pira l'orrendo foco' (The horrible fire of the funeral pyre...). For a detailed consideration of the imagery of light and fire in Alfieri's *Agamennone* see D. O'Grady 'Exaltation et destruction de la Raison dans la tragedie *Agamennone* d'Alfieri', in I. Mamzcarz (editor), *Théâtre de la crueté, théâtre de l'espoir*, Collection Théâtre Européen, Klincksieck, Paris, 1996, pp. 77-85.

30 A. Boito, *Otello*, op.cit., p. 12.

31 See H. Busch (editor), *Verdi's 'Otello' and 'Simon Boccanegra'* in Letters and Documents, op.cit., pp. 485-6.

32 Ibid.

33 See Shakespeare, Othello, Arden Shakespeare, Methuen, London, 1959, p. 55.

34 H. Busch (editor), Verdi's 'Otello' and 'Simon Boccanegra' in Letters and Documents, op.cit., p. 485.

35 Theologically this represents some conflict, since Otello is seen to be essentially good. This introduces a further argument which does not concern us at this point: are Jago and Otello the products of the same God or Scientific experiment?

36 A. Boito, *Otello*, op.cit., p. 25

37 See Chapter II, p.36.

38 Ibid.

39 A. Boito, *Otello*, p. 25

40 A further dimension of Boito's 'duality' is seen here: the just man is a liar and so false. The evil, sincere and so true. Boito has thus reversed the moral order, with evil becoming good, and good becoming evil.

41 A. Boito, Otello, op.cit., p. 30.

42 It may well be argued that Desdemona as Oliba in *Re Orso* and *Gioconda* of Boito's libretto *La Gioconda*, (written under the pseudonym Tobia Gorria, for Ponchielli), represents Venice, pure and stainless, but the victim of ambitious assault by virtue of her position.

43 A. Boito, *Otello*, op.cit., p. 28

44 Ibid., p. 29

45 There is clear evidence of the influence of Alfieri's Egisto (*Agamennone*) on Boito's Iago. Alfieri's persona, in turn owes much to his Shakespearean model, the villain hero of *Othello*.

46 Note that the Italian 'coscienza' means both 'conscience' and consciousness. This co-existence of awareness and moral discernment will later be explored by Luigi Pirandello.

47 A. Boito, *Otello*, op.cit., p. 29

48 Ibid., p. 37

49 See Shakespeare, *Otello*, op.cit., p. 103

50 A. Boito, *Otello*, op.cit., p. 29. Baldacci points out that the passion is presented in terms of an experiment. See   L. Baldacci, *La musica in Italiano*, op.cit., p. 88.

51 See L. Baldacci, La musica in Italiano, op.cit., p. 251: Boito is the first of Italian intellectuals to do without an   idealogy, almost warning that the moment of technique has arrived and that all idealogies are good provided that they allow for a laboratory experiement.

52 See Shakespeare, *Othello*, op.cit., pp. 119-20.

53 A. Boito, *Otello*, op.cit., p. 39

54 Ibid., p. 65

55 Ibid., p. 66. One notes that Otello has been transformed from a symbol of Venice, the winged lion, to a (winged) fly caught in a web of intrigue.
56 Ibid., p. 53
57 Ibid., p. 69
58 Ibid., p. 77
59 Ibid., p. 78
60 See *La Gioconda*, with libretto by Boito, under the pseudonym of Tobio Gorria. In her suicide aria, 'Suicidio' Gioconda makes reference to the final gesture on her path.
61 A. Boito, *Otello*, op.cit., p. 78.
62 Ibid.

CHAPTER 4

The Puppet Show

The introduction to this study stresses the link between the beautiful and ugly, the good and evil, constantly engaged in expressions dominated by emotion and pathos, given lyrical and dramatic reality through the communication of laughter and tears. The cult of the ugly was probed, and dramatized thematically and with psychological connotation by Victor Hugo in *Le roi s'amuse*. The ugly form or rather deformity gave way to the destruction of the accepted literary form and formula.[1] Laughter was enforced; it provoked tears and resulted in the identification of the grotesque with the pathetic. In an act of self justification it became evil, but paradoxically was also the father of beauty and goodness. In Francesco Maria Piave's adaptation of *Le roi s'amuse* for Giuseppe Verdi, the fusion of genre was central to the interpretation of the work: Jester and man set up an internal struggle for supremacy: the man attempts to avenge the Jester, after a series of self-analytical considerations. The jests and exchanges that are traditionally part of the Jester's repertoire, and are seen as conversations with the bauble, containing the effigy of the Jester's own head, are transformed to an internal debate with the self, in which the conscious and sub-conscious assume gigantic proportions.[2] Evil conquers, as is reflected in the undoing of father and daughter, and the psychological implications of a curse. Yet, in a world beyond human comprehension and scientific dexterity, good, the child of evil, can pray for and redeem the erring father. When Arrigo Boito highlighted the death of traditional art, by grotesquely presenting it in an incomplete ('Un torso') or mutilated form ('Lezione d'anatomia') he pointed to the deconstruction of the object, in order to reinvent a means of expression which might incorporate harmony of image through visual and musical enunciation. In many respects *Re Orso* looks both backwards and forward, without any real resolution of the contradiction presented in such a statement. It refers back to the absurdity of Romantic idealism. It reinforces the destruction of brute force. In destroying pure poetry (Oliba), it points to the need for a new series of poetics, based on new harmonic forms, which can best be expressed through music and drama. This is demonstrated through his own attempts as poet and composer. With the failure of *Amleto* and the success 'd'estime' of *Mefistofele*, it became apparent that the unqualified success of such an artistic expedition could only be realised through the collaboration of separate powers: those of the poet and musician. Boito's *Otello* became the successful realization of this plan. At face value *Otello* ranks as an unqualified tragedy. The conflict between laughter and tears is not immediately apparent. There would not appear to be a fusion of genre. Yet in relation to Cassio, a sinister approach to laughter is introduced. His drinking song evolves as a parody on the more conventional drinking songs by Piave i.e. 'Libiamo, libiamo' of *La Traviata* and 'Si colmi il calice' of *Macbeth*, although a duplicity of purpose is present in the latter. The purpose of the piece introduced by Iago and echoed by the chorus is to discredit Cassio in the eyes of Otello and to create disharmony.[3] It is indirectly the source of the lyrical love duet, with which it contrasts poetically. However the 'kiss motif' which closes the first act on a note of tenderness is also that which closes the opera, when the tragedy has been completed. In other words, lyrically, and thematically the drinking son and Cassio's later drunken laughter are in sharp contrast to the poetic harmony associated with the love of Otello and Desdemona. Inane laughter is the source of the ultimate tragedy. The calculated 'Ride chi vince' (He who wins laughs), *Otello*, I, 1. of Jago, and Cassio's response 'Vince chi ride' (He who laughs wins), introduces sinister and irrational laughter. It carries the concept of laughter and tears from the romantic settings of Hugo and Piave to the macabre indication of psychological derangement in Luigi Pirandello's *Il berretto a sonagli*. Here the Jester's enforced laughter and licence to make others laugh is replaced by Ciampa's 'Orrible risata di rabbia, di selvaggio piacere e di disperazione a un tempo (horrible laughter of anger, primitive pleasure and dispair), *Il berretto a sonagli*, II, 5. Having forced Beatrice Fiorica to wear the Jester's cap of feigned madness, Ciampa gives way to the laughter of insanity and despair.

By the end of the nineteenth-century the romantic treatment of the pathetic in literature had yielded to the realism of the grotesque. Scapigliatura and its poetic confrontation of Art and Science had provided a gentle revolution after which nothing in terms of poetic expression and artistic philosophy could remain the same. The concept of laughter and tears and their ironic connotations had been touched upon as early as 1824 by Giacomo Leopardi. In 'Elogio degli uccelli',[4] he ironically declares that man, of all creatures, although the least happy, is the only one capable of laughter. This, he maintains can be explained in the following terms: man originally laughed in drunkenness, which provided an escape from his misery. In 1856 Francesco De Sanctis, considering the crisis of Romanticism considered humour in the following terms: Beffarsi di tutte le regole...L'umore non vuol dire il capriccio, l'arbitrio, la licenza, il puro illimitato...Esso ha per iscopo l'illimitato... L'umore è una forma artistica, che ha per suo significato la distruzione del limite con la coscienza di essa distruzione...L'umore ha per sua essenza la contraddizione.[5] (To make fun of all rules...humour does not mean a whim, the taking of liberty, licence, the mere unlimited...it has for its object the limitless. Humour is an art form that has for meaning the destruction of limits with the consciousness of such destruction.) [6]

With scientific progress, and the application of Science to human behaviour, the theory of laughter became the subject of philosophic discussion and speculation. A series of European publications pave the way for the Pirandellian combination of literary and scientific principles, subjected to contradiction, which result in the parody of older forms, in the service of psychological realism. Fundamental to the ideological appreciation of Pirandello's black comedy *Il berretto a sonagli* are the following works: H. Bergson, *Le rire* (1899); T. Massarani, *Storia e filosofia dell'arte di ridere* (1900-2); J. Scully, *Essai sur le rire* (1904); G.A. Levi, *Il comico* (1913); A.F. Formiggini, *Filosofia del ridere* (1907).[7] In 1908 Pirandello published an essay on humour – 'L'umorismo'. This draws on De Sanctis' concept of making fun of regulations and of creating and destroying. There emerges a concept of Art which has as its essence contradiction.[8] However, Pirandello does not follow in the footsteps of those who had determined a need for digression in taste (as indeed did the members of Scapigliatura). To quote G. Tellini, he provided structures with the mechanical precision of a clock: Pirandello è giunto a disgregare l'immagine unitaria della realtà: a rappresentare non solo il dramma che si fonda sul contrasto tra sostanza e apparenza, tra verità e finzione, ma quello della multipla fenomenologia delle apparenze sottentrate alla sostanza, il dramma dello sgretolamento della "verità", della "realta".[9] (Pirandello demolished the unified vision of reality in order to not only present the drama based on the contrast between substance and appearance, truth and invention, but also the multiple phenomenon of the appearances replacing fact, the drama of the disintegration of 'truth' and 'reality'.)

What critics have however failed to recognize or rather register is the progression from the deconstruction of the physical and artistic in the works of Hugo, Piave and Boito, to Pirandello's analytical deconstruction of behaviour and destruction of the psyche, resulting in the dramatization of madness. As does Boito's *Otello*, Pirandello's black comedy *Il berretto a sonagli* centres around the supposed infidelity of a wife and the male's approach to such a situation. As Piave and Boito, Pirandello operates a psychological duality of reason/madness, truth/appearances, freedom/imprisonment. As in the case of *Otello*, there evolves a drama of suspicion and doubt, with psychological implications. Since in Boito's drama one witnesses the point to point expression of uncertainty provoked by sexual jealousy, one is consistently aware of the troubled thoughts of the protagonist, their motivation and succession. Boito develops his drama from within and without. One is aware of cause, effect and the sequence of psychological progressions which result in the final act of violence. Otello is the 'primitive' or 'essential' man. His torment is an essay on the vulnerability of the human psyche caught between personal and professional dealings, in a society based on male dominance. Otello is not however mad; rather in today's social climate he would be described as psychologically disturbed.

Ciampa in Pirandello's comedy demonstrates throughout an unhealthy preoccupation with the human psyche, from his projection of individuals as puppets, to his exposition of the theory of the three strings. Pirandello's psychological progressions are thus externalized in terms of the movement and manipulation of marionettes. The mind, controlled by the brain, is seen as similar to a clock with its pendulum and three strings. As the strong manipulates the least strong, Pirandello modifies the scale on which actions and reactions may be perceived. Individuals, dehumanized are made to conform to social convention. In such a society, both power and position are held by the puppet master, irrespective of his or her social status. On such an individual rests the power to convert the spontaneous initiative of any group to a puppet show. In ceding to the miniature and isolating incidents and behaviour patterns, Pirandello is both highlighting and mocking social convention. Its slaves *are* no more than puppets, manipulated by strings and in need of public applause.

I believe that a line in Piave's *Rigoletto* provides a link between the drama of doubt and suspicion conducted between servants and masters in the three works under scrutiny. As Rigoletto muses on his relationship with his master, the Duke of Mantua, he exclaims:

> Questo padrone mio
> giovin, giocondo, si possente, bello,
> Sonecchiando mi dice,
> Fa ch'io rida, buffone.[10]
>> *Rigoletto*, Act I, 8.

> (This master of mine,
> young, joyful, so powerful, handsome,
> sleepily says to me.
> Make me laugh, jester...)

Later Rigoletto, in the presence of Gilda calls himself 'Solo, difforme, povero (alone, deformed, poor). As Ciampa, the servant clerk, considers his superior the Cavaliere, we are reminded of the words of Triboulet (Hugo) and Rigoletto (Piave):

> Perchè uno tante volte...poniamo, brutto, vecchio, povero...
> che può saper lei, signora...con quale supplizio questo
> vecchio può sottomettersi fino al punto di spartirsi l'amore di quella
> donna con un altro uomo –giovane. ricco, bello. [11]
>> *Il berretto a sonagli*, Act II, 5.

(Because one, very often, let us say ugly, old, poor...you can understand, madam, with what torment that old man can humiliate himself to the point of sharing the love of that woman with another man...young, rich, handsome.)

In both dramas an old, poor and unattractive servant must yield to a young, handsome and rich master. In each case the master appears to succeed in gaining the old man's most cherished possession: Rigoletto's daughter, Caimpa's wife. While every detail of the action is clear in *Rigoletto*, Pirandello leaves much space for speculation. Otello's doubts however are unfounded. He does not lose his wife to another man but sacrifices his peace of mind:

Ma, o pianto, o duol! M'han rapito il miraggio
Dov'io giulivo, – l'anima acqueto.[12]

Otello, Act III. 3

(But, oh tears, oh suffering they have stolen the mirage
which made me joyful–peace of mind.)

The dramatic and poetic works under discussion, serve to illustrate the thematic variations which literature underwent in the second half of the nineteenth and early twentieth century. The crisis of form and content is exemplified by means of the shifting from a social and artistic ideal to a reconstruction of the real. The Jester is proven to be powerless, but the Artist and puppet master may construct reality according to their wishes. In *Il libro dei versi – Re Orso*, Art is seen as the victim. In *Otello*, Beauty, innocence and poetry falls at the hands of the Science of evil. In the Sicilian society of *Il berretto a sonagli*, truth is sacrificed to convention by means of the progression from truth to appearances. The credible yields to the absurd. Although truth and madness are initially seen to occupy opposite poles, at the conclusion of the work madness is regarded as a rational solution. It is the only means by which truth may be expressed. The folly of the Jester who voluntarily wears the cap with bells of madness, has become the frustration of the individual forced to wear the same cap to protect those whose conventions cannot accept an unpleasant truth. Further detail and clarification is called for. A detailed study of the work reveals Pirandello's debt to Boito: whereas Boito parodies form, character and object by degrading and ridiculing, Pirandello comes full circle by overturning and updating the genre, society and character in order to demonstrate the absurdity of a female Jester enforced to perform the role of mad woman in order to protect the traditional ethos of Sicilian society. Such thematic and literary variations evolved in Pirandello's case, in a post-futurist society when both technology and the autonomous scientifically regulated object had become the subject of literature. *Il berretto a sonagli*[13] was written in dialectic form in 1916, with the title *A birritta cu i ciancianeddi*. It is based on two short stories, 'Certi obblighi'[14] and 'La verità'[15] which appeared in *Corriere della sera* in 1912. Staging the work presented difficulties on account of the localized form of the dialect, and the heated

96

verbal outbursts against the male-oriented society depicted in the work. Pirandello worked on the language of the comedy until it came to reflect the dialect spoken in and around Catania. He also made some cuts to the text before it was performed in June 1917 at the Teatro Nazionale, Rome. Although its success was no more than moderate, it was absorbed into the repertoire of the dialectic theatre. The Italian text of the comedy appeared in the journal *Noi e il mondo* in 1918, and in 1920 was published by Trèves. It finally reached the stage of the Teatro Morgana, Rome in 1923, where it was performed by the Monaldi company. Thus in the space of seven years it went from the status of local expression to a nationally accepted piece of theatre. With the publication and performance of the work in Italian, it not only reached the Roman public but was on its way to becoming internationally received. Meanwhile, the Sicilian version was continuing to impress local audiences and in 1936 it was presented in Neapolitan, with Eduardo De Filippo as Don Nociu Pàmpina, who became Ciampa in *Il berretto a sonagli*. In 1965 the autographed manuscript of the original version was discovered by Alfredo Barbina. In 1984, Luigi Squarzina restored the cuts which Pirandello had made in deference to the Sicilian public. This finally allowed the original version of the work be published and performed. This is the version of the Mondadori edition of 1986, reproduced by the Foundation for Italian Studies, University College Dublin.[16]

At face value the work is concerned with regionalistic codes and how they touch a well-to-do society, geographically and intellectually isolated from the social changes which touched a greater part of Italy in the early part of the twentieth century. It demonstrates male dominance and the place of the 'delitto d'onore' or 'crime of honour' in the penal and behavioural codes of the time. With its translation into Italian it assumes many more social, literary, philosophical and psychological attributes. It encapsulates and condenses all possible attitudes of mind as regards the possible and probable adultery of a couple from diverse social backgrounds. In the absence of consolidated facts however, there exist mere suspicion and doubt. The plot is as follows: Beatrice Fiorìca suspects that her husband, the Cavaliere is having an affair with the wife of his clerk, Ciampa. In an attempt to prove their infidelity, she sends Ciampa on an errand to buy a necklace, similar to one she suspects her husband may have bought for Nina Ciampa. Beatrice hopes that the couple will take advantage of Ciampa's absence, and sends the forces of law and order to his house. Although the Cavaliere is present, his behaviour is not compromising, and no real proof can be found against them. However news of the events has spread throughout the neighbourhood. Ciampa feels his manhood threatened and an unwritten law demands a 'crime of honour' in order to restore his status within his own community. In order to avoid this, and nonetheless protect his own personal image, he decides that Beatrice Fiorìca must feign madness. In this way the situation is saved: all believe (or pretend to do so), that the accusation was the result of the wife's insanity. The sole sufferer is the outspoken woman, who must repair to a mental institution.

The theme of insanity is one which occupied Pirandello in his private life and also as part of his literary output. In 1903 his wife, Antoinetta Portulano suffered a psychic collapse which developed into an incurable illness. Her paranoia and persecution complex forced Pirandello and his three children (toward the end of 1918) to commit her to a neurological clinic in Rome, where she lived until the end of the Second World War. Writing in the *Giornale d'Italia* of May 8, 1924, Pirandello claimed to comprehend the psychology of those alienated in body and mind from the social environment. Madness then, became a source of inspiration for Pirandello.[17] In *Enrico IV*, written in 1921, and first performed in the Teatro Manzoni, Milan, in 1924, the dramatist provides a portrait of one who believes himself to be the eleventh-century Emperor. The illusion, caused by a riding accident, was accepted by his family and society in order to placate the pathetic individual. When, however, twelve years later, the subject recovers his reason, he continues to live with his illusion, realizing that his 'real' life had escaped him, and that illusion had become his reality. As Marco Manotta states:[18] 'in the drama, there is not a trace of 'neurological' disorder since, by the time the 'persona' appears, he has accepted madness as a philosophical solution to his problems. As soon as he is called upon to justify it, he leaves the stage'.

In *Non si sa come* (1934) Romeo Daddi becomes mad, on realizing his inability to comprehend and rationalize his behaviour. The fear of losing his reason leads to an intensity of rationalisation which carries the mind to its extremity and thus madness. It is also however manipulated as a defence against the loss of self control. Beatrice Fiorìca (*Il berretto a sonagli*) is forced to act mad, in order to defend social hypocrisy. It is the author's way of stating: only the 'mad' can be truthful, spontaneous and sincere. By refusing to consciously behave as a puppet, she allows her strings to be pulled in the opposite direction, to that in which she believes to argue.

From physical and artistic deformity, as the source of realistic pathos (Piave)

98

and poetic parody (Boito), Pirandello provides deformity of mind in a philosophical, psychological and ironic register. His philosophical[19] and ideological sources, in addition to the literary forms discussed, are to be found in Freudian thought and the futuristic promotion of the 'machine'.[20] His technical prowess is in no small extent due to his overturning and parodying literary and theatrical genres with which his public and readership would have been well acquainted.

The concept of the human being as a puppet, a wooden doll drawn and manipulated by strings, is along with madness an outstanding feature of *Il berretto a sonagli*. Marco Manotta in his study *Luigi Pirandello*,[21] reminds us that early in the twentieth century H. von Kleist had imagined a puppet theatre, not susceptible to the laws of gravity. In 1907, F.M. Marinetti in *Poupées électriques* explains the hypocrisy of social convention in terms of static marionettes, which he makes to symbolize human destiny. In the same year G. Craig in *L'attore e la super-marionette* proposed the puppet as the model of a substitute for the actor in order to transcend the psychological drama, and to provide the director with an object which could be controlled, in terms of movement and expression. At the same time the puppet theatre represented an innocence associated with childhood. In some of his short stories Pirandello evokes childhood memories of the arrival of the puppeteer (*La Scelta, Paura del sonno, Favola del figlio cambiato*). In a letter to his sister Lina, Pirandello exclaimed that life appeared an enormous incomprehensible puppet show. ('Osservando la vita sembra un'enorme pupazzata, senza nesso, senza spiegazione mai.')[22] As the century progressed the puppet lost its connotation with innocence, and became the externalization of man, his mirror image, or even his double. There are references to marionettes in *I giganti della montagna* and *Come tu mi vuoi*.[23] In *Il berretto a sonagli*, the puppet expresses the eclipse of the will and the absurdity of human spontaneity. The story does not end here however, as Rosso di San Secondo's *Marionette, che passione* (1919) demonstrated a spontaneity and individualism, which was expressed by the distortion of the puppet form as it sought to reach beyond the limits devised by its makers.[24] It may be concluded that Pirandello absorbed the literary and scientific associations with puppets, with which the early twentieth century abounded. He clearly draws inspiration from the diverse literary functions of puppets in the half-century preceding his writing *Il berretto a sonagli*. The form evokes innocence, manual manipulation and scientific progress. One recalls the conflict of Art, Nature and Science in the tales of E.T.A. Hoffmann. The presence of the mechanical doll, in the opera *Les*

contes d'Hoffmann (Offenbach, 1881), after the play by Barbier and Carré, founded in turn on the stories of Hoffmann has implications in the area of both sex and
Science.[25] In the first tale, Hoffmann is in love with the mechanical doll, Olympia.
The second story finds him in the arms of the Venetian courtesan Giulietta. The
consumptive Antonia in the third tale, who is too frail to sing, dies when forced to
do so by an evil magician. The doll, a mechanical and beautiful object, breaks. The
calculating courtesan feels no more sincere passion than the former, and leaves by
gondola in the company of a dwarf. Olympia, the mechanical doll is the product of
scientific invention, a cross between the innocent human reproduction of the self
and a sexual object. Although breakable, one must bear in mind that in Hoffmann's
tale, she is broken, smashed in a fit of rage by one of her inventors. Hoffmann's
doll is the production of a sophisticated new world looking towards the triumph of
the machine and technological progress. Pirandello's puppets however, combine
the primitive world of folk tradition with the Freudian findings on the subconscious
and psychoanalytical. Pirandello's puppets in *Il berretto a sonagli* are not mechanical. They are theoretical and exist only in a hypothesis of comparison. They are
moved by strings, and they provide an illustration of Pirandello's theory of the
three strings of human behaviour. They, like their doubles are mindless, mere
objects in the hands of a clever human manipulator. Like Olympia in the opera,
they can be broken, when the codes of Sicilian convention are infringed. Beatrice
Fiorìca, by attempting to expose the suspected adultery of her husband with
Ciampa's wife, destroys the social image of the betrayed party. Effectively, as
Ciampa states (Act II,4), 'she has trampled upon his image, his self respect, in a
word his 'pupo'.' Ciampa physically demonstrates this by trampling on his own
hat, a further symbol of social decorum and self respect:

Ciampa:	Sua sorella non ha fatto altro che prendere il mio nome – il mio pupo – ... – il mio pupo: buttarlo a terra e sopra – una calcagnata – così.![26] *Butta il suo cappello in terra e lo pesta col piede.*
Ciampa:	(Your sister has done nothing but take my name – my puppet...my puppet, throw it on the ground and trample on it – like this!) *He throws his hat on the ground and stamps on it with his foot.*

100

In order to regain his self-esteem Ciampa must become puppet-master. In declaring Beatrice mad, he is in fact pulling her 'corda pazza' (mad string) and in the event becomes both manipulator of reason and psychiatrist. By pulling Beatrice's 'mad string', Ciampa is effectively smashing her puppet image. Pirandello is at pains to demonstrate the individual 'psychologically smashed' is in effect succumbing to a mental collapse. The broken 'pupo' reveals both the loss of self-esteem and psychological stability. These become totally identified in Pirandello's world. In its social and geographical isolation it is a puppet theatre parodying the 'bel mondo' or 'high society' of the Sicilian provinces. Pirandello thus identified reason/madness and the puppet world. This philosophical and psychological dimension is absent from the world of 'La verità'. The local customs and social conventions are seen to be similar in both pieces. In *Il berretto a sonagli*, Pirandello has added diverse levels of significance and interpretation. In combining the philosophical and the grotesque, he provides a comedy of the absurd which carries a social and psychological message valid for present day readers and public. In the short story, 'La verità', the wronged husband has actually killed his unfaithful wife and the entire piece centres around his interrogation in a Sicilian courtroom. The story demonstrates the disclosure of fact, which is consistently linked with the term 'truth' (la verità) in such a way that there is no conflict between popular belief, evidence and the words of the accused. Fact is indeed true. If the word is written, then is must be so. It must be true. This reflects the credulity of the uneducated Sicilian classes. The sole conflict exists between the intentions of the defence lawyer and Tararrà, the protagonist. The former argues that the offence was the result of a spontaneous outburst of anger. The latter, insists on the truth, introducing the accusation of Signora Fiorìca and thus demonstrating that the act was premeditated. Pirandello achieves his effect by combining fact with irony: Io abito in campagna, Eccellenza. Ma se in codeste carte sta scritto, che ho ammazzato mia moglie, è la verità. E non se ne parla più.[27]

(I live in the country, your Excellency. But if in these papers it is written that I have murdered my wife, it is the truth. And there is no more to be said.)

The confession of guilt, is in effect a statement of innocence, but unlike the manner of presentation in the later Pirandello, when opposites are philosophically justifiable, the effect here is merely comical: l'ho falto propriamente, Signori giurati, perchè non ho potuto far di meno, ecco, e basta.[28] (I actually did it, gentlemen of the jury, because I had to, there it is and that's all.) The real 'guilt' is attributed to Signora Fiorìca for having spoken of such things: La colpa è stata della signora...che non ha voluto lasciar le cose quiete.[29] (It was the Signora's fault...that did not want to keep things quiet.)

The position of the wronged wife is ignored, or rather ridiculed, her presence is realistically drawn: con le dita piene d'anelli, le gote tinte di uva turca, e tutta infiocchettata come una di quelle mule che recano, a suon di tamburo, un carico di frumento alla chiesa.[30] (With her fingers full of rings, her cheeks coloured with grapes, and all decked out like one of those donkeys that, to the beat of a drum, carries a load of wheat to the church.)

The ridicule of the betrayed husband is accorded both irony and pathos: Ma non ha pensato vissignoria, che c'era un altro uomo di mezzo?[31] (But had your worship not considered that there was another man involved?)

With regard to ingredients then, 'La verità' contains the background to what will become *Il berretto a sonagli*: an illicit affair, an outspoken wife and a betrayed husband, with all the social implications of the latter state. The story demonstrates the victory of fact, devoid of psychological implications. Tararà denies any logical thesis, protesting the truth, and consequently is condemned to thirteen years imprisonment. The shifting in emphasis from mere statement to the rational progression of thoughts is touched upon by Leonardo Sciascia in his study *Pirandello e la Sicilia*..[32] He argues that the communication of opposites takes place within the character, rather than outside of it as is the case with Tararà of 'La verità'. This leads to the resolution of the situation, through rational sophistication.

The second source of *Il berretto a* sonagli, 'Certi obblighi' shows the justification of restraint, in the case of a betrayed husband Quaquèo. As the town lamplighter, he cannot abandon duty and plunge the town into darkness, in order to spy on his wife, and later if necessary to kill her: Bella scusa, l'illuminazione della città, per sottrarsi all'obbligo di badare ai torti della moglie.[33] (A fine excuse, the lighting of the lamps, for disposing of the obligation of taking care of his wife's misdemeanours.) Unlike Tararà, a loutish peasant, Quaquèo has rationalized his situation. Pirandello has introduced reason, at the level of parody, and it may be concluded that he is preparing the way for Ciampa of *Il berretto a sonagli*. The contrast between light and darkness symbolizes the conflict between knowledge and ignorance or rather feigned ignorance. Yet paradoxically by lighting the town, and avoiding it remaining in darkness, he assumes that he is kept in the dark with regard to his wife's actual movements. The lamps thus, are object symbols, communicating enlightenment, and enlightened civic spirit, while the semantic 'ragionare' (to reason/rationalize) is provided at the opening of the story: Quest'uomo...deve contrarre la cattiva abitudine di ragionar con se stesso.[34] (This man must take on the bad habit of reasoning with himself.) The entire piece thus evolves as a parody on enlightened thought. The final revelation is that Quaquèo's betrayer is his social superior, a Cavaliere.[35] In the two stories, Pirandello provides primarily an admission and acceptance of social codes in a male dominated society. He juxtaposes truth and appearances, knowledge and ignorance. In 'Certi obblighi' he externalizes the light of reason in the form of the symbolic lamp in order to illustrate its presence and significance, and the stupidity of his protagonist. The effect is that reason is critically applied by the reader, in order that he/she interpret the tale at both a social and philosophical level. With the combination of the technical variations seen in the stories 'La verità' and 'Certi obblighi', Pirandello in *Il berretto a sonagli* achieves a masterpiece in black comedy and both a factual and philosophical acccount of human reactions.

Il berretto a sonagli is Pirandello's sole two-act piece for the theatre. The structure of the play, the scene divisions and the number of characters all represent the author's projection of his theme through the external form. The concepts of order, balance and lack of equilibrium are communicated through both structure and content, semantic and theme throughout the play. The order in which characters appear is also of symbolic significance, as is also the space (both temporal and textual) allocated to them. In Act I, Beatrice, as social superior attempts to control the situation. In Act I, scene 4, in his confrontation with her, Ciampa speaks in 'generale' (in general) and expounds his theory of the three strings. Act I stands as a theoretic exposition of Science and social possiblities. In Act II, scene 4, when Ciampa effectively takes control of events and the eventual destiny of Beatrice, his conversation focuses on the 'particolare' (particular), as he practically applies his behavioural theory. The balance thus between theory and practice is demonstrated by means of the even division of the acts.

One is however aware on closer observation, that Act I, which contains Ciampa's theoretic approach is made up of six scenes. Act II, on the other hand, with its attempted rationalization of madness, is made up of five scenes. Adding up to the uneven number eleven, they demonstrate numerically the social and psychological imbalance demonstrated within. Although the social superior is female, she must yield to the manipulations of a male servant. Pirandello integrates and contradicts the traditional war between the classes, to finally replace it by one between the sexes. This is further demonstrated when one considers the gender of the personae: there are eight in all, five of which are female, and three of which are male. Nonetheless, the victory is finally with the male members of the cast, as the defence of the 'pupo' (puppet) dictates. Pirandello's play, in its original dialectic form, was an exposition of local customs and their preservation. The great absentee in *Il berretto a sonagli* is the Cavaliere, around whom the drama centres, and whose movements are as dubious as is the existence of the necklace Beatrice instructs Ciampa to buy.[36]

As a comedy in which servants and masters are seen to be in conflict (one is aware not only of Beatrice's conflict with Ciampa, but also, with Fana, her servant who attempts to make her listen to reason), Pirandello's updating and overturning the eighteenth century enlightened comedy of Goldoni emerges. Set in the home, or salon of a wealthy provincial family, it takes the form of a conversation piece on the art of social decorum. However Pirandello gently parodies the upper classes. The Cavaliere may possess a title, but not the sword of the eighteenth-century nobility. He is the twentieth-century's answer to the eighteenth-century enlightened aristocrat: he is a symbol of financial prowess and enconomic progress. Being a Banker, he represents power and authority, yet his social position is by no means unique. As already stressed, Ciampa's theory of the three strings and his description of the cast as puppets equates the entire series of events with a puppet-show. Yet Pirandello would appear to parody the traditional puppet theatre. This represented chivalric tales of Knights and Ladies (Donne e Cavalieri). The Knight, traditionally the defender of the social and moral code, is a far cry from the Cavaliere Fiorìca, who by his absence, does nothing to defend his Lady Beatrice from ridicule and humiliation. The figures surrounding Beatrice: Fana, La Saracena, Fifì, Assunta, Spanò resemble *Commedia dell'Arte* stock figures and provide an initial front against Ciampa and later against Beatrice. They represent society, the chorus, and the collective justification of local convention.

If one considers the order in which the characters appear and speak in Act I, it is clear that Pirandello has planned his dramatic strategy mathematically. Fana, a servant, yet rationally attempts to advise the hysterical Beatrice. However, La Saracena occupies the space between them. As scene I. progresses the characters speak in diverse order. In the entire scene, there are twenty nine exchanges. Of this uneven number of dramatic interventions, the longest speech is that of the emotional La Saracena. In a battle between reason and emotion for the mind of the one who blesses (Beatrice), Pirandello parodies the philosophic treatises of eighteenth-century literature and drama.[37] It is clear that the emotional dimension will carry the day. Beatrice later, as the victim of her emotional disposition, will prove victim of the logic of insanity.

Act II, scene 1, the order of appearance of Fana and Beatrice is reversed. The former is accorded merely one line of dismay on hearing the sound of the door bell, and the possible arrival of the forces of law and order:

Beatrice: Voglio esser fuori prima di sera!

               Via da questa casa maledetta!

               Si ode una scampanellata alla porta.

Fana: Oh madre di Dio, e chi sarà.[38]

Beatrice: (I want to be out before evening.

               Away from this damned house.

               A ringing at the door is heard.

Fana: Oh Mother of God, who can it be?)

Fana, as Reason, practicality and common sense is caught between Beatrice's first illogical exposition of her wishes and her calculated expectation of the arrival of Spanò.

Structurally Pirandello has conveyed the message of the play by means of the distribution of Acts, scenes and characters and order of appearances. The themes of reason/madness, truth/appearance, certainty/doubt contribute to the creation of a drama of jealousy and suspicion, in which a verbal joke becomes a fact. The linking of the theory of the three strings, the projection of the puppet and the enforcement of madness as a rational solution are effected in Act I, scene 4, and Act II, scenes 4 & 5. In the course of the two expositions in scene 4 of each act, Ciampa, as a result of a symbolic fall, passes from the exponent of social theory to a broken man, seeing all in reverse. Yet, as one discovers, his eyes are unharmed,[39] merely his glasses or the means of interpretation of his vision have been damaged. In the final scene, a Sicilian solution to a Sicilian problem is found.

The three principal symbolic images of the work are the hypothetical necklace, the puppet and Ciampa's spectacles. The necklace may be identified with suspicions within the plot. It eventually becomes identified with the source of the plot. The puppet is the symbol of self-respect within the plot, while the spectacles, as in Hoffmann's *Der Sandmann* and Offenbach's *Contes d'Hoffmann* are the means by which the puppet is perceived and interpreted. References to Ciampa's eyes, sight and his spectacles are made in Act I,4 in conjunction with the exposition by Ciampa of the theory of the three strings. This is closely followed by Ciampa's projection of the puppet. At once the presence of theoretic psychology is established, with the working of the human mind considered, not from within, but from without. The association with an inanimate object makes for visual clarity but as the point is pressed, the association becomes less convincing and less absolute.[40] The application of the theory is effected through the description of the social image of the puppet, which is arrived at by means of a consideration of alternatives. The physical description of Ciampa provided by Pirandello presents a figure of about forty five years of age. The entire description,with the exception of the fact that he wears a frock-coat, centres on his head, the source of the strange rationalizations which he is about to present.[41] His hair is drawn back but untidy. He has no moustache but wears two broad sidelocks, which reach as far as underneath his 'occhi pazzeschi' (mad eyes) which are hard and sharp in expression, and dart back and forth behind his 'pince-nez' spectacles. Behind his right ear he carries a pen. From such a portrait, his quick thinking mind and penetrating glance are communicated. Ciampa arrives on a physical errand which demonstrates his frame of mind. He comes to express through insinuation his concern for his wife Nina's reputation and his need to keep her under lock and key. This is to make Beatrice aware that she is not in the company of her husband in the absence of Ciampa:

Ciampa: ed è mia
           cura che non vada per le bocche della gente...[42]
                        Il berretto a sonagli, Act I, 4.

Ciampa: (And I am
           anxious that she shall not be the subject
           of people's conversations...)

Ciampa converts Beatrice's words to insinuations to the point where it would appear that the characters are competing with each other, in order to establish a fact in the mind of the other, without making a direct statement:

Ciampa: Lei vuol farmi intendere sotto le parole
                 qualche cosa che la parola non dice.[43]
                              Il berretto a sonagli, Act I, 4.

Ciampa: (With the use of words, you wish to convey something
                 that words don't say.)

Each character is aware of the other's suspicion. In competing for control, each is vying for supremacy. Ciampa would wish to speak 'seriamente' or 'seriously' and privately with Beatrice. On the refusal of the latter to admit her understanding of Ciampa's words, he feels forced to speak correctly and civilly:

Ciampa: Soprattutto, dovendo vivere in società,
                 ci serve la civile; per cui sta qua, in mezzo
                 alla fonte. ...
                 Ma può venire il momento che le acque
                 s'intorbidano. E allora...allora io cerco,
                 Prima, di girare qua la corda seria, per chiarire.
                 Rimettere le cose a posto, dare le mie ragioni...
                 ...se poi non mi riesce in nessun modo,
                 Sferro, signora, la corda pazza, perdo la vista
                 degli occhi e non so più quello che faccio![44]
                              Il berretto a sonagli, Act I, 4.

                 (Above all, having to live in society, the string
                 of decorum is
                 necessary; for that reason it is here,
                 in the middle of the
                 forehead...
                 But the moment may come when waters become muddy.
                 And then...I try, before pulling here, the string of seriousness,

to clarify things, put them in order, make my case.

And then, if I can't succeed on any account, Madam,

I pull the mad string –

I lose my eyesight and no longer know what I am doing.)

Ciampa's explanation of behaviour is perfectly clear. The symbolism of the clock has been clarified. However, yet another dimension co-exists alongside the literal and the symbolic. This is the philosophical, which has been subtly introduced from the beginning of the play in terms of aspects of reason and madness, allied to consciousness and understanding. Beatrice in scene 1, is described as 'isterica' (hysterical). Her sexual jealousy is apparent from the outset. In Act I, 4, she asks Ciampa if he is so jealous as to become suspicious at the mere mention of his wife's name. In Act I, 6, she admits to being jealous. When Beatrice insists that she wishes to speak 'seriamente' 'seriously' to Ciampa, she reminds him that she is truly serious:

Beatrice:	Non sto mica parlando per ischerzo.[45]
	Il berretto a sonagli, Act I,4.
Beatrice:	(I am not speaking for a joke.)

One notes thus that hysteria and jealousy may be viewed as a forerunner to madness, while a joke or jest is madness, or abandonment of reason on purpose, or for fun. In Act II, 5, the term 'scherzare' is used with more sinister undertones. Ciampa refuses the pity and ridicule of his acquaintances who might utter, in jest:

Ciampa:	Non è stato nulla, Ciampa: la signora ha scherzato.[46]
	Il berretto a sonagli, Act II,5.
Ciampa:	(It was nothing Ciampa, Madam was joking.)

When Ciampa declares that he will kill the adulterous couple, Fifì and Spanò enquire:

Fifì e Spanò:	Ma siete pazzo? Chi ammazzate?[47]
	Il berretto a sonagli, Act II,5.
Fifì and Spanò:	(But are you mad? Who will you murder?)

The company attempt to convince him that it was all mere madness – 'una pazzia'. With the chorus of 'madness', Ciampa concludes that all can be remedied if Beatrice is declared mad. Reason had been introduced, with reference to motivation: Beatrice's motivation in calling Ciampa to her presence.[48] Ciampa in turn, had wished to speak 'seriamente': 'dare le mie ragioni.' The rational conclusion in order that the family of Ciampa and the Cavaliere avoid disgrace is to have the outspoken nuisance Beatrice put away. The social dimension allied to that of knowledge and truth is ironically included in Ciampa's accommodation of facts:

Ciampa: Basta che lei si metta a gridare in faccia
                       a tutti la verità. Nessuno ci crede, e
                       tutti la prendono per pazza.[49]
                             Il berretto a sonagli, Act II, 5.

Ciampa: (It is sufficient that she shout the truth to
                       everyone. No one will believe her, and all
                       will take her for mad.)

The philosophical and psychological are thus identified in the interest of social respectability.

The term 'coscienza' meaning both conscience, with moral implications, and consciousness, awareness or understanding, is introduced at the beginning of the play. The semantic 'coscienza' also plays a role in indicating that the play is not, as in the case of *Otello*, the manipulation of an innocent, by a diabolical raisonneur. Rather that it represents two knowing and calculating individuals attempting to control a compromising situation. In Act I, scene 1, 'coscienza' is pronounced six times in the debate between Fana and La Saracena, before the introduction of the term 'vero' (true) into the exchange between the two women. When Beatrice utters the word, it is in answer to the question:

Beatrice: è vero che il padrone prima che da
                       Catania doveva passare da Palermo?[50]
                             Il berretto a sonagli, Act I,4.

Beatrice: (Is it true that the master before going to Catania
                       had to pass through Palermo?)

From this point 'coscienza' yields to more definite form 'sapere': Perchè so, che sapete?...che non sapete nulla.[51] (Because I know,...what do you know?...you don't know anything.) With the reference to the hypothethical necklace the relationships between fact and knowledge, belief and truth become blurred, as the drama develops on two levels: as one of doubt and suspicion and as one of refined calculation, as Ciampa takes posession of the entire stage in scene 4 of both acts. Ciampa's presentation of society as populated by puppets provides the cultivation of a self-image which must be publically supported. As the puppet develops as an alter ego, it not only proves to be the externalization of the self, but also demonstrates a certain independence, as it takes delight in the social respect which it inspires. Pirandellian irony has paradoxically demonstrated the freedom of the individual once it has accepted that its behaviour *outside* of the family home must be in accordance with the social decorum associated with the 'corda civile' or string of civility or decorum. The puppet however, as the necklace, has no *actual* existence. If the former owes its linguistic presence to the ill-intended gossip of La Saracena and the credulity of Beatrice, the puppet is a metaphor for social hypocrisy. Although its self-respect may be undermined, on account of its having no acutal or material reality, it cannot be torn apart or smashed as Olympia, the mechanical doll of *Les Contes d'Hoffmann*. The presentation and triumph of the puppet is seen in Act I,4. Its humiliation is demonstrated in Act II,4. The following piece illustrates the freedom to design one's own puppet, or choose one's own mask:[52]

Ciampa: Pupi siamo, caro signor Fifì
            ...ognuno poi si fa pupo per conto
            suo: quel pupo che può essere, o che si erede
            di essere.[53]

Ciampa: (We are puppets, dear Mr Fifi.
            Each one makes himself a puppet in his
            own way: that puppet that he can be, or that he
            believes to be.)

Spontaneity is destined for life beyond the view of neighbours.[54] The war between husband and wife puppets must be abandoned, as they set about a performance for the public. Here the neighbours or acquaintances become a mere audience to a puppet show:

110

Ciampa: La guerra è dei due pupi: il pupo –
                 marito e la pupa moglie. Dentro si strappano i
                 capelli...appena fuori però,si mettono
                 a braccetto...corda civile lei, corda civile
                 lui, corda civile tutto il pubblico...e i
                 due pupi godono, trionfi d'orgoglio e di
                 soddisfazione.[55]

Ciampa: (There is war between the two puppets: the
                 puppet-husband and the puppet-wife. Inside
                 they tear each others hair out...as soon
                 as they go out they link arms: the civil string
                 for her, the civil string for him, the civil string
                 for the whole public...and the
                 two puppets enjoy triumphs of pride and
                 satisfaction.)

In Act II,4, Ciampa is seen to enter in disarray: his forehead cut, his collar unbuttoned and his tie loosened. He carries his spectacles in his hand. His sole explanation is that he has broken them. He later explains that his puppet has been trampled upon. His self-image shattered, on account of the public knowledge of the reported affair between his wife and the Cavaliere Fiorìca, he appeals only to Beatrice's conscience or consciousness:

Ciampa: Una sola domanda volevo rivolgerle,
                 e non alla Signora propriamente, ma alla sua
                 coscienza.[56]

Ciampa: (I wished to ask her a single question, and not of
                 the Signora herself, but her conscience.)

The contradictory nature of the evidence against the apparently adulterous couple sums up the inability of the individual to define truth or certainty. They were found to be 'insieme e non insieme' (together or not together), or rather together but not in the expected sense. Ciampa's comment on the situation would apparently mean,

'I can see what is going on behind my back (io guardo in terra e conto le stelle, anch'senz'occhiali), I look to the ground and count the stars, even without my glasses'. Pirandello has however, linguistically indicated that nothing is to be found where one might expect to find it. Ciampa, having hit his head is seeing stars. They are however seen to be on the ground! In other words, all order has been reversed and overturned. This symbolic reversal of the order of vision points to the contradictory conclusion of the work. The same ambiguity accompanies Ciampa's statement to Assunta in Act II,5:

Ciampa: Non è niente, signora. Il guajo è per
               gli occhiali, che mi sono rotti, Ci vedo e
               non ci vedo. Ma, tanto ormai, non ho più
               niente da vedere.[57]

                         Il berretto a sonagli, Act II,5.

Ciampa: (It is nothing, Madam, The problem is as
               regards my spectacles, that I have broken.
               I see and I don't see. But at this point there
               is nothing more to be seen.)

Pirandello is using the verb 'vedere' to illustrate sight and understanding. 'I see and I don't understand.' He may however be blinded with anger, but there is no more to be seen.[58] His sight is here identified with life: to all accounts he has now nothing to live for. The damaged spectacles have protected Ciampa's eyes, sight and psychological vision. His forehead may be bruised but unlike in his father's case (Act I,4),[59] it is not shattered. His diabolically sophisticated plan can be carried to completion.

Mention has been made earlier in the chapter of the presence of parody throughout the play. As a social comedy of manners and errors, it ridicules with ironic precision many of the features of the eighteenth-century 'beau-monde'. In keeping with the lessons in wit and logic imparted by Harlequin, and other such clever servants[60] , Pirandello has allowed the comedy conclude as a lesson in behaviour. In place of the 'School for lovers', 'School for Wives', or 'School for Scandal', he has provided a 'School for Madness', with Beatrice as pupil and Ciampa as teacher. His lesson points to the illustration of the behaviour of the mad,

112

and it is followed by an assessment of the reaction of the subject Beatrice. The application of such a lesson is demonstrated, with the pupil shouting its convictions and appearing truly mad. The teacher laughs with pleasure and despair. Ciampa's lesson is based on an acceptance of a thesis: that Beatrice is mad. Such a fact must be made general knowledge:

Ciampa: E lo sappiamo tutti qua, che lei è pazza.
                   E ora dove saperlo tutto il paese.[61]
                                Il berretto a sonagli, Act II,5.

Ciampa: (And we all hear now, that she is mad.
                   And now the entire neighbourhood must know it.)

                   ...Gliel'insegno io come si fa, Basta che
                   lei si metta a gridare in faccia a tutti la
                   verità. Nessuno ci crede, e tutti la prendono
                   per pazza![62]
                                  Il berretto a sonagli, Act II,5.

                   (I shall teach you how to do it. All you have to
                   do is to shout the truth at everyone. No one will
                   believe it, and everyone will take you for mad.)

Beatrice's response that she is right, that she is sane and that Ciampa knows that this is so, is followed by a question mark. (Ah dunque voi lo sapete che io ho ragione...?) (Ah so you know that I am right?). Her control is seen to crumble, as she effectively makes a statement by asking for reassurance. Ciampa continues the lesson by referring to a hypothetical page in a lesson-book:

Ciampa: Volti la pagina signora! Se lei volta la
                   pagina vi legge che non c'è più pazzo al mondo
                   di chi crede d'aver ragione.[63]
                                  Il berretto a sonagli, Act II,5.

                   (Turn the page Signora, if you turn the page, you read
                   that there is no one in the world madder, than the person
                   who believes to be right, to be rational.)

113

Beatrice is told to avail of the opportunity of speaking the truth. Ciampa, as a man, in the society in which he lives is unable to do so. He would like to give free expression to his feelings, as a man, as may Beatrice as a woman. He not only envies Beatrice's possibility of expressing herself, but claims that it will prove beneficial to her health. The lesson is completed without the consent of the pupil. In many respects the learning process is parodied. Neither intellectual facts or values are imparted. The lesson may be said to be absorbed in an unruly manner and applied in a demonstration of anti-social behaviour. Consumed by anger Beatrice applies the truth, not in order to clarify matters, but to further insult Ciampa and trample on his puppet:

Beatrice: Sì Bèèè, ve lo grido in faccia,
               sì bèèè.[64]

                              Il berretto a songali, Act II, 5

Beatrice: (Yes, Cuckold. I'll shout it at you
               yes, cuckold.)

As she repeats the word with increasing frustration and anger, the mad scene is enacted. The salon comedy demonstrating the victory of a clever servant has not only provided an assessment of sexual jealousy and its approximation to madness, but has also illustrated the narrowness of the boundaries between two apparently opposite states of mind. The plot then, may be determined in philosophical terms. The two principal characters, Beatrice and Ciampa in association and contrast with one another actively demonstrate the psychological process involved in creating and preserving self-esteem. If the work, on another level may be regarded as a parody of eighteenth-century salon comedy, it is also necessary to point out that the world of Goldoni, gently caricatured and parodied a world of reason and refinement as expressed through manners and mannerisms. The comical vision of the age of Reason, with enlightenment cultivated in popular terms, amongst the servant class, sought to consolidate, by means of criticism, a society in the service of Reason. Pirandello on the contrary, cruelly decries a world in which truth can only be stated in apparent madness. He allows Ciampa manipulate reason, in order that it yield to madness. But he might also wish to illustrate, as does Boito in *L'alfier nero*, that reason having completed its calculations, may indeed succumb to emotional pressure, resulting in madness. Ciampa's unhealthy preoccupation with the human psyche, its unnatural projection as an inanimate object and his manipulation of and experimentation with emotional reaction has resulted in a breakdown in expression. Following the semantic *pazza – pazza* (mad–mad), his words give way to a horrible outburst of laughter that can only lead to the questioning of Ciampa's own psychological stability.

NOTES

1   Comedy and tragedy were made to exist as part of a single work of art.

2   At this point in the development of connotations of the self, the grotesque is expressed through the bauble, which is the externalization of the jester's mind and form.

3   Social, poetic and musical disharmony are in fact effected.

4   G. Leopardi, *Operette morali*, Rizzoli, Milan, 19 pp.

5   F. De Sanctis, 'Giornale di un viaggio nella svizzera durante l'agosto del 1854', *La crisi del romanticismo. Scritti dal carcere e primi saggi critici*, Einaudi, Turin, 1972, pp. 540-42.

6   See 'La linea umoristica', G. Tellini, *Il romanzo dell'Ottocento e Novocento*, op.cit., pp. 82-8.

7   See A.F. Formiggini, *Filosofia del ridere*, edited by L. Guicciardi, Clueb, Bologna, 1989.

8   L. Pirandello, *L'umorismo ed altri saggi*, edited by E. Ghidetti, Giunti, Florence, 1994.

9   G. Tellini, *Il romanzo dell'Ottocento e Novecento*, op.cit., p. 262.

10   F.M. Piave, *Rigoletto*, op.cit., p. 19.

11   L. Pirandello, *Il berretto a sonagli*, J.C. Barnes (editor), Belfield Italian Library, Foundation for Italian Studies, University College Dublin, 1990, pp. 100-101.

12   A. Boito, *Otello*, op.cit., p. 47.

13   See J.C.Barnes (editor), *Il berretto a sonagli*, op.cit., pp. 11-12.

14   See L. Pirandello, *Novelle per un anno*, vol. I, Mondadori, Milan, 1939, pp. 1187-94.

15   Ibid., pp. 590-97.

16   See introduction, J.C. Barnes, *Il berretto a sonagli*, op.cit., pp. 11-44.

17   See E. Gianola, *Pirandello e la follia*, Il Melangolo, Genoa, 1983; J.M. Gardiar, *Pirandello e il suo doppio*, Abete, Rome, Bruno, 1977; M. Manotta, *L. Pirandello*, Mondadori, Milan, 1998, pp. 103-6.

18   M. Manotta, *L. Pirandello*, op.cit., p. 103.

19   See G. Andersson, *Arte e teoria. Studi sulla poetica del giovane Pirandello*, Almquist and Wicksell, Stockholm, 1966; A. Iliano, *Metapsichica e letteratura in Pirandello*, Vallecchi, Florence, 1982; M. Lavagetto, *Freud, la letteratura e altro*, Einaudi, Turin, 1985; F. Orlando, *Per una teoria Freudiana della letteratura*, Einaudi, Turin, 1973; O. Rosati, *'Il berretto a sonagli' di Pirandello, attraverso Moreno e Freud'* in O. Rosati (editor), *Pirandello e lo Psicodramma in Italia*, Ubaldini, Rome, 1982, pp. 62-77; See also: G.P. Biasin, *Malattie mentali*, Bompiani, Milan, 1976; G. Jung, *La schizofrenia*, Boringhieri, Turin, 1977; Th. Szasz, *Il mito della malattia mentale*, Il Saggiatore, Milan, 1908.

20   See G. Livio, *Il teatro in rivolta, Futurismo, grottesco, Pirandello e pirandellismo*, Mursia, Milan, 1976; S. Milioto/S. Scrivano (editors), *Pirandello e la cultura del suo tempo*, Mursia, Milan, 1984; R. Tessari, *Il mito della macchina. Letteratura e industria nel primo Novecento italiano*, Mursia, Milan, 1973.

21   M. Manotta, *Luigi Pirandello*, op.cit.

22   See *Lettere ai famigliari*, in 'Terza programma', 3, Turin 1961, p. 281.

23   See D. Radcliff-Umstead, 'Pirandello and the Puppet World', Italica, 44, 1967, pp. 16-19. Also S. D'Amico, *Il teatro dei fantocci*, Vallecchi, Florence, 1920.

24 See Pirandello's reaction to the work in *L. Pirandello Saggi, Poesie, Scritti Varie,* edited by M. Lo Vecchio-Musti, Mondadori, Milan, 1960, pp. 1007-9.

25 The episode concerning the doll Olympia is taken from Hoffmann's *Der Sandmann* (1817). For an account of the tale see: H.W. Hewett-Thayer, *Hoffmann, Author of the Tales,* Princeton University Press, Princeton, New Jersey, 1948, pp. 186-88; H.S. Daemmrich, *The Shattered Self,* Wayne State University Press, Detroit, 1973, pp. 47-51. The dominant themes considered are the imagery of the eyes, the shattered self and the puppet.

26 L. Pirandello, *Il berretto a sonagli,* op.cit., p. 98.

27 L. Pirandello, *Novelle per un anno,* op.cit., p. 593.

28 Ibid., pp. 593-4.

29 Ibid., p. 594.

30 Ibid., p. 592.

31 Ibid., p. 597.

32 See L. Sciascia, *Pirandello e la Sicilia,* Adelphi, Milan, 1996, pp. 60-66. See also E. Licastro, *Luigi Pirandello dalle novelle alle commedie,* Fiorini, Verona, 1974, pp. 17-35. Pirandello's technique in converting the prose of short-stories to dramatic form is also treated of in P. Briganti (editor*), L. Pirandello. Dalle novelle al teatro,* Mondadori, Milan, 1990. It does not however discuss *Il berretto a sonagli.*

33 L. Pirandello, *Novelle per un anno,* op.cit., p.1187.

34 Ibid., p.

35 Riccardo Bacchelli in his comedy *La famiglia di Figaro* also uses the symbol of lamplighting in order to parody the ancient regime of the Enlightenment. Doctor Bartolo the symbol of the old order in Beaumarchais' trilogy and Da Ponte's *Le nozze di Figaro,* in Bacchelli's comedy is entrusted with the illumination of the city.

36 The fact that the Cavaliere is not seen on stage contributes to the uncertain impression created re: his movements, his purchases and his intentions.

37 The tragedies of V. Alfieri consistently project a symbolic battle between reason and emotion.

38 J.C. Barnes (editor) *Il berretto a sonagli,* op.cit., p. 86.

39 Pirandello in common with Hoffmann treats of the protection of the eyes and the symbolism of glasses. See Hoffmann *Der Sandmann.*

40 See N. Bonifazi, *Teoria del fantastico e il racconto fantastico in Italia,* op.cit., p. 20.

41 *Il berretto a sonagli,* op.cit., p. 70. The concentration on the description of the head – the container of thoughts and reflections is also a device present in Manzoni's *I promessi sposi* and Verga's 'Cavalleria Rusticana'.

42 *Il berretto a sonagli,* op.cit., p. 71.

43 Ibid., p. 72.

44 Ibid., p.73.

45 Ibid.

46 Ibid., p. 102.

47 Ibid.

48 Beatrice in sending Ciampa away from home, was effectively leaving the way clear for her hus-

band and his wife to meet.

49 *Il berretto a sonagli*, p. 105.

50 Ibid., p. 65.

51 Ibid.

52 It is noteworthy that Ciampa's 'lessons' in behavioural science are directed at Fifi, Beatrice's brother, whom he eventually convinces of the effectiveness of his plans. This may be interpreted as an illustration of male solidarity, regardless of differences in social background.

53 *Il berretto a sonagli*, op.cit., p. 75. Note Pirandello's reversal of the usual form 'Siamo pupi'. This marks the beginning of a series of reversals and inversions by Ciampa.

54 It is also to be noted that Beatrice will be allowed to *behave* as a madwoman, in the institution to which she is committed. If true freedom is seen to be madness, it is however freedom of *expression* which is achieved. Beatrice is deprived of her *physical* freedom on account of her verbal indescretions.

55 *Il berretto a sonagli*, op.cit., pp. 75-6. One is reminded of the domestic violence in the Punch and Judy Show.

56 *Il berretto a sonagli*, op.cit., p. 98.

57 Ibid., p. 99.

58 Ciampa, having pulled the 'mad string' is demonstrating what was said in Act I,4. 'Perdo la vista degli occhi, e non so più quello che faccio.' His vision is not permanently damaged, as only his spectacles, which may be repaired, are broken.

59 *Il berreto a sonagli*, op.cit., p. 74.

60 Figaro, of the Beaumarchais triology, *Le barbier de Seville* (1775), *Le mariage de Figaro* (1778) and *La mère coupable* (1791), is an example of an enlightened servant, protecting the honour of women, in a battle of the sexes.

61 *Il berretto a sonagli*, op.cit., p. 105.

62 Ibid.

63 Ibid.

64 Ibid., p. 106.

Conclusion

By focusing on the three writers whose works are analysed, compared and contrasted in this study, it has been my intention to illustrate the decomposition of form, during the post-Romantic era. By accepting the co-existence of the beautiful and the ugly, good and evil, the romantic and realistic, Hugo not only introduced and accepted a contradiction in terms, but by means of the hunchback-Jester Triboulet, presented deformity as the subject of a work of art, representing life. The role of the Jester, vacillating between the forces of light and darkness, truth and falsehood provokes a debate on the function and philosophy of laughter, which will develop towards the close of the century. With the adaptation of *Le roi s'amuse* by Francesco Maria Piave the tragedy of deformity is individualized. Alongside the more conventional interpretations of the text, the deformity of the poetic text is introduced. This is aided by Piave's utilization of the traditional Arcadian poetic expression, alongside a new, more modern and psychologically oriented form. With the tragedy developing in terms of the poetic miniatue and the larger-scale grotesque, a new dramatic formula is introduced. In Act I the image of the head of the Jester, reproduced on his bauble, his own self-analytical reflections, the introduction of decapitation and Rigoletto's opening lines: 'Ch'avete in testa, Signor di Ceprano?' provide an introduction to a drama in which the realistic and psychological unite.

Arrigo Boito, in the *Libro dei versi*, in search of artistic innovation, juxtaposes creativity and destruction. In considering Nature and Art in its essence, the essential duality of human activity emerges. It embraces Good and Evil, Light and Shade, Belief and Negation, but finds its most elementary outlet in the service of nature by Art and Science. Art, and poetry in particular fall victim to scientific manipulation, analysis and dissection, as seen in 'Lezione d'anatomia'. In an attempt to create a more complete and purer art form, Boito advocates the identification of literature and the figurative arts with music. In 'Un torso' he provides a headless torso, decapitated by time, and adds the reflections of the poet in order to complete an artistic whole. In *Re Orso*, the decapitation of Oliba, leads to her return to nature: she is the moon, celebrated in the song of the troubadour, itself a parody of Leopardian lyricism. Throughout the polymetrical *Re Orso* Boito is experimenting with metre, poetic form and parody of poetic convention. The destruction of conventional expression, and the parody of traditional subject-matter points towards a new poetic genre, expressive of and allied to musical form.

Botio's *Otello* not only provides a new series of poetics, combined with an operatic reform, but it also applies the theory of 'Dualismo' with the introduction of a psychological dimension. The human form, in this case Otello, is scientifically programmed towards a psychological collapse, which in turn will destroy the traditional expression of poetic beauty, innocence and orthodox religious belief symbolized by Desdemona. Since the final result is tragedy, Boito would appear to decry the demon of his own creation. Jago, with his scientific playing on human emotion emerges as an evil psychiatrist. Although the poetic *persona* is destroyed, the *form* is revitalized at the conclusion, with the repetition of the 'kiss' motif of the 'love duet', which represents a new affintiy between the harmony of words and melody.

While Boito provides a theoretic approach in his poetry and *Re Orso*, he reproduces a drama of internal struggle in *Otello*. Pirandello provides the externalization of such a debate. While Piave illustrates the deformity of the human form and its symbolic connotations and Boito shows the brutal and grotesque in an attempt to decry tradition, Pirandello shows madness as a deformity of mind. *Rigoletto*, *Otello* and *Il berretto a sonagli* centre on suspicion, doubt and their relationship to infidelity. *Rigoletto* opens with insinuation, in order to provoke. *Otello* is a drama of insinuation. *Il berretto a sonagli* demonstrates the subtle meeting of minds through insinuation and its psychological effect. Pirandello's theoretic and scientific realism transforms the human being to a mere puppet: a symbol of self-respect and self-gratification. In an era when the mechanically operated object was seen to express a new-found freedom, or a predictability which robbed it of its spontaneity, Pirandello provides the more traditional puppet form, operated by the strings of a clever puppet master. This demonstrates the Science of behaviour which can have primitive or sophisticated attributes. In providing an analysis of human behaviour, based on acts both rational and irrational, Pirandello provides a dramatized essay on Reason and Madness. On probing the various layers of consciousness: knowledge, belief, doubt, suspicion and combining them with mental activity such as imagination, invention, and exaggeration, Pirandello effectively deconstructs the human psychological process. Complexity is achieved by the addition of literary devices associated with earlier literary movements i.e. enlightenment, romanticism and realism. The irony of such associations lead in turn to humour, parody and the absurd. Yet it is clear that Pirandello is providing an advanced 'dualismo' or 'duality', albeit a scientifically oriented one. The conflict between Reason and Madness is played out with regard to two characters in a two act play. This contains central terms open to dual interpretation: Ragione (reason, cause), coscienza (conscience, consciousness), vero (true, actual). The essential conflict projected on a *dramatic* level is between Ciampa and Beatrice. Philosophically speaking however, it is between man and his puppet which emerges as his double and self-image. This is in effect between his true self and the self 'remodelled' for social purposes. Such contrast negates the 'true self' and expresses the antithesis of the situation created in *Il fu Mattia Pascal*. In the latter the protagonist rejects his enforced identity, in order to embrace the purer form of self, which is in fact unattainable. In *Il berretto a sonagli* an accommodation is arrived at as Ciampa opts for his puppet, and Beatrice, obliged to accept his manipulation, allows the mad string to be pulled. At this point it becomes clear that duality may also be applied to the puppet itself: it is open to voluntary or imposed manipulation in the spectacle of life.

It may be argued that human deformity in Hugo and Piave, and the deconstruction and re-assembly of the poetic form in Boito, is carried by Pirandello to a new dimension, with the introduction of the conscious and subconscious. The Sicilian dramatist operates from within and without the dramatic persona. As artist and master of letters, he carries the comic world to a new literary level. As scientific thinker he explores the secrets of the psyche and exposes them in such a manner as to create a distance or gap between the 'dramatis persona' on stage and its puppet or double. The unity of the individual may then be said to be destroyed. Its ingredients and constituents have been analysed to the point where their dramatic reality and presence is undermined. The destruction of the puppet is however, merely the destruction of a concept. Unlike Hoffmann's mechanical doll it has no *material* presence. Pirandello has invented an alternative persona, which can exist merely as a literary and philosophical concept.

The study of Piave and Boito, does I believe, illustrate a literary revolution which took place back stage, rather than on the centre stage of Italian drama. I believe they provide the fundamental links from the Romantic to the Realistic, which have yet not been acknowledged. Their relationship to twentieth-century Modernism is fundamental. The Scapigliatura Milanese has often been regarded a small revolt, by a small number of artists giving rise to a small number of secondary works. It is an undeniable fact however, that after the advent of Arrigo Boito nothing in the field of literary theory and practice was as before. His analysis of the self and of poetics, and his application of *poetic science* to his *artistic* output changed the face of Italian literature.

BIBLIOGRAPHY

Abbiati, F., *Verdi*, Ricordi: Milan, 1959.

Alonge, R., *Pirandello tra realismo e mistificazione*, Guida: Napoli, 1972.

Altieri Biagi, M.L., 'Pirandello dalla scrittura narrativa alla scrittura scenica' in *Lingua e scena*, Zanichelli: Bologna, 1980.

Andersson, A., *Arte e teoria. Studi sulla poesia del giovane Pirandello*, Almquist & Wicksell: Stockholm, 1966.

Andre, A., *Taccuino segreto/Luigi Pirandello*, Mondadori: Milan, 1997.

Angelini, F., *Il teatro del Novecento da Pirandello a Fo*, Laterza: Rome/Bari, 1976, pp. 34-8.

Apollonio, M., *Storia della Commedia dell'Arte*, Sansoni: Florence, 1982.

AA.VV., *Pirandello e il teatro*, Palumbo: Palermo, 1985.

Baldacci, L., *La Musica in italiano: Libretti d'opera dell'Ottocento*, Rizzoli: Milan, 1997., *Libretti d'opera ed altri saggi*, Vallecchi: Florence, 1974.

Baldini, G., *Abitare la battaglia*, Garzanti: Milan, 1970.

Barbina, A., *La biblioteca di L. Pirandello*, Bulzoni: Rome, 1980.

Bettini, F., *La critica e gli scapigliati*, Zanichelli: Bologna, 1976.

Biasin, G.P., *Malattie mentali*, Bompiani: Milan, 1976.

Billington, S., *A Social History of the Fool*, The Harvester Press: Sussex; St Martins Press: New York, 1984.

Binni, W., *L'Arcadia e il Metastasio*, Sansoni: Florence, 1963.

Bonifazi, N., *Teoria del fantastico e il racconto fantastico in Italia: Tarchetti-Pirandello-Buzzati*, Longo: Ravenna, 1982.

Borsellino, N., *Storia di Verga*, Laterza: Bari, 1992.

Budden, J., *The Operas of Verdi*, I, Cassell: London, 1973.

Busch, H., (editor), *Verdi's 'Otello' and 'Simon Boccanegra' in Letters and*

Documents, Clarendon Press: Oxford, 1988.

Busi, A., *'Otello' in Italia, 1777-1972*, Laterza: Bari, 1973.

Caesar, A., 'Construction of Character in Tarchetti's *Fosca* in *The Modern Language Review*, 82, 1987.

Calendoli, G., 'The Theatre of the Grotesque' in *Drama Review*, 77, March 1978.

Carnazzi, C., 'Verga e i veristi', in SLIV, *L'Ottocento*, III, 1997, pp. 2179-292.

Cesari, G., & Luzio, A., (editors), *I copialettere di G. Verdi*, Stucchi Ceretti: Milan, 1913.

Sozzi-Casanova, A., *La Scapigliatura*, Cooperativa libreria I.U.I.M.: Milan, 1979.

Cornuz, J., *Hugo, l'Homme des Misérables*, Favre: Lausanne, 1985.; *Hugo, l'Homme des Misérables*, Editions Piene-Marcel Favre: Paris, 1985.

Crotti, I/Ricorda.R., *Scapigliatura e dintorni*, Vallardi: Milano, 1992.

Daemmriott, H.S., *The Shattered Self,* Wayne State University Press: Detroit, 1973.

Davenport-Hines, R., *Gothic. Four Hundred Years of Excess, Horror, Evil and Ruin,* Fourth Estate: London, 1998.

D'Amico, S., *Il teatro dei fantocci,* Vallecchi: Florence, 1920.

Debenedetti, G., *Verga e il naturalismo,* Garzanti: Milan, 1976.

Del Nero, D., *A. Boito: un artista europeo,* Olschki: Florence, 1995.

Del Principe, D., *Rebellion, Death and Aesthetics in Italy. The Demons of Scapigliatura,* Associated University Presses: New York, 1996.

De Rensis, R., (editor), *Lettere di Arrigo Boito,* Società Editrice 'Novissima", Rome, 1932.

Descotes, M., 'Du drame à l'opera: les traspositions lyrique du théâtre de Victor Hugo', in *Revue d'histoire du théâtre 34:* 1982, pp. 103-56.

Di Pietro, A., *Per una Storia della letteratura italiana postunitaria,* Vita e pensiero: Milan, 1974.

Doran, J., *A History of Court Fools,* London, 1855.

Esslin, M., *The Theatre of the Absurd,* Penguin: London, 3rd edn. 1980.

Felver, C.S., *Robert Armin: Shakespeare's Fool,* Kent State University Bulletin: Kent, Ohio, 1961.

Farinelli, G., *Dal Manzoni alla Scapigliatura,* Istituto Propaganda Libraria: Milan, 1991.

Formiggini, A.F., *Filosofia del ridere,* edited by L. Guicciardi, Clueb: Bologna: 1989.

Franceschetti, G., 'La fortuna di Hugo nel melodramma italiano dell'Ottocento', in *Contributi dell'Istituto di Filologia Moderna, serie francese,* II, Università Cattolica del Sacro Cuore: Milan, 1961.

Garzilli, E., "Between the circle and the Labyrinth: Mask, Personality and Identity in Pirandello" in *Circles without a Centre,* Harvard University Press, Cambridge, 1972.

Genco, G., *La morte della persona e la nascita del personaggio,* Mandoria: Lacaita, 1993.

Ghidetti, E., (editor), *L. Pirandello, 'Umorismo' ed altri saggi',* Giunti: Florence, 1994.

Gianola, E., (editor), *La Scapigliatura,* Marietti: Turin, 1975.; *Pirandello e la follia,* Il Melangolo: Genoa, 1983.

Giazotto, R., 'Hugo, Boito e gli Scapigliati' in *L'approdo letterario* – luglio-sett, 1958.

Giovanelli, P.D., *Gino Gori: Il grottesco e altri studi teatrali,* Bulzoni: Rome, 1978.

Gori, G., *Il grottesco nell'arte e nella letteratura - comico, tragico, lirico,* Stock: Rome, 1926.; *Scenegrafia. La tradizione e la rivoluzione contemporanea,* Stock: Rome, 1926.

Granatella, L., "Per una interpretazione della Scapigliatura", in *Otto/Novocento,* gen.febbr. 1981, n.1, pp. 177-183.

Gronda, G., & Fabbri P., *Libretti d'opera italiani: dal Seicento al Novocento,* Mondadori/Meridiani: Milan, 1997, introduction pp. Xi-LIV.

Gulino, G., "Il teatro dialettale di Pirandello: 'A birritta cu'i ciancianeddi', in *Pirandello dialettale,* edited by S. Zappulla Muscarà, Palumbo: Palermo, 1983, pp. 160-73.

Hepokoski. J.A., *Giuseppe Verdi's 'Otello',* Cambridge University Press: Cambridge, 1987.

Howett-Thayer, H.W., *Hoffmann, Author of the Tales,* Princeton University Press: Princeton, New Jersey, 1948.

Iermano, T., (editor), *Positivismo, Naturalismo, Verismo, Questioni teoriche e analisi critiche,* Vecchierelli, Manziana: Rome, 1996.

Iliano, A., *Metapsichica e letteratura in Pirandello,* Vallecchi: Florence, 1982.

125

Isella, D., 'Approccio alla Scapigliatura' in *I Lombardi in rivolta*, Einaudi: Turin, 1984, pp. 231-9.

Jung, G., *La Schizofrenia*, Boringhieri: Turin, 1977.

Kayser, W., *The Grotesque in Art and Literature*, Indiana University Press: Bloomington, 1963.

Kerr, W., *Tragedy and Comedy*, Da Capo, New York, 1968.

Lavagetto, M., *Boito, Opere*, pp. VII-xxxvIII, Garzanti: Milan, 1979.; *Freud, la letteratura e altro*, Einaudi: Turin, 1985.

Lea, K.M., *Italian Popular Comedy: A Study in the Commedia dell'Arte*, Oxford University Press, Oxford, 1934.

Livio, G., *Il teatro in rivolta. Futurismo, grottesco, Pirandello e pirandellismo*, Mursia: Milan, 1996.

Luzio, A., (editor), *Carteggi verdiani*, 4 vols. Reale Accademia d'Italia: Rome, 1935-47.

Macchia, G., *Pirandello la stanza della tortura*, Mondadori, Milan, 1981.

Madrignani, C.A., *Capuana e il naturalismo*, Laterza: Bari, 1970.; *Regionalismo e naturalismo in Toscana e nel Sud: Collodi, Pratesi, Capuana, De Roberto, Serao*, in LIL, VII/l, 1975, pp. 511-63.

Manotta, M., *Luigi Pirandello*, Mondadori: Milan, 1998.

Marim, V., *A. Boito fra Scapigliatura e classicismo*, Loescher: Turin, 1968.

Mariani, G., *Storia della Scapigliatura*, Sciascia: Rome, 1971.; "Le varianti di A. Boito", in *Ottocento romantics e verista*, Napoli, 1972.; "Il melodramma della Scapigliatura", in *Il Dramma* agosti-settembre 1971 and also in *Ottocento romantica e verista*, Naples, 1972, pp. 279-290.

Marotti, F., & Romei, G., *La Commedia dell'arte e la società barocca: la professione del teatro*, Bulzoni: Rome, 1991.

Martinello, L., *Lo specchio magico*, Dedalo: Bari, 1992.

Mila, M., *L'arte di Verdi*, Einaudi: Turin, 1980.

Molinari, C., *La Commedia dell'arte*, Mondadori: Milan, 1985.

Morelli, G., (editor), *Atti del Convegno Internazionale di studi dedicato al centocinquantesimo della nascita di A. Boito*, Olschki: Florence, 1994.

Milioto, S., & Scrivano, E., (editors), *Pirandello e la cultura del suo tempo*, Mursia: Milan, 1984.

Musitelli Paladini, M., *Nascita di una poetica: il verismo,* Palumbo: Palermo, 1974.

Nardi, P., (editor), *A. Boito, Tutti gli scritti,* Mondadori: Milan, 1942.; *Vita di A. Boito,* Mondadori: Milan, 1942.; *Scapigliatura (Da Giuseppe Rovani a Carlo Dossi),* Mondadori: Milan, 1968.

Nencioni, G., "Parlato–parlato, parlato–scritto, parlato-recitato," in *Strumenti critici,* 1976, X, pp. 1-56.

O'Grady, D., *The Last Troubadours. Poetic Drama in Italian Opera,* 1597-1887, Routledge: London/New York, 1991.

Orlando, F., *Per una teoria freudiana della letteratura,* Einaudi: Turin, 1973.

Osborne, C., *Rigoletto – A Guide to the Opera,* Barrie & Jenkins: London, 1979.

Petronio, G., *Dall'illuminismo al verismo,* Manfredi: Palermo, 1962.

Petrucciani, M., *Emilio Praga,* Einaudi: Turin, 1962.

Pompeati, A., *Arrigo Boito, poeta e musicista,* Battistelli: Florence, 1919.

Powers, H., 'Boito rimatore per musica' in G. Morelli (editor), *Arrigo Boito: atti del Convegno Internazionale di studi, dedicato al centocinquantesimo della nascita di A. Boito,* Fondazione Giorgio Cini: Venice, 1994.

Quadrelli, R., 'Poesia e verità nel primo Boito' in *Arrigo Boito poesie e racconti,* ed. Rodolfo Quadrelli, Oscar Mondadori: Milan, 1981.

Radcliffe-Umstead, D., 'Pirandello and the Puppet World', *Italica,* 44, 1967, 13-27, pp. 16-19.; "Pirandello: The destruction of the social Marionette", in *Dimensioni,* 1973, nn. 1-2.

Radice, R., (editor), *Eleanora Duse/Arrigo Boito. Lettere d'Amore,* Il Saggiatore: Milan: 1979.

Ragusa, O., *Pirandello, an approach to his Theatre,* Edinburgh University Press: Edinburgh, 1980, pp. 76-81.

Ricci, C., *Arrigo Boito,* Trèves: Milan, 1924.

Rosa, G., *La narrativa degli Scapigliati,* Laterza: Rome/Bari, 1997.

Rosati, O., "*Il berretto a sonagli* di L. Pirandello attraverso Moreno e Freud" in *Pirandello e lo psicodramma in Italia,* Ubaldini: Rome, 1982, pp. 62-77.

Rossi, S., *L'età del verismo,* Palumbo: Palermo, 1978.

Salvetti, G., "La Scapigliatura Milanese e il teatro d'opera" in AA.VV., *Il melodramma italiano dell'Ottocento,* Einaudi: Turin, 1977, pp. 567-604.

Sciascia, L., *Pirandello e la Sicilia,* Adelphi: Milan, 1996.

127

Smith, P., *The Tenth Muse*, Gollancz: London, 1971.

Sormani, E., *Bizantini e decadenti nell'Italia umbertino*, Laterza: Rome, 1975.

Spera, F., *Il principio dell'antiletteratura, Dossi, Faldella, Imbriani,*, Liguori: Naples, 1976.

Spinazzola, V., *Verismo e positivismo*, Garzanti: Milan, 1977.

Szasz, Th., *Il mito della malattia mentale*, Il saggiatore: Milan, 1980.

Taviani, F., & Schino, M., *Il segreto della Commedia dell'arte*, Casa Usher: Florence, 1982.

Tedeschi, R., *Addio Fiorito asil: Il melodramma italiano da Boito al verismo*, Studio Tesi, Pordenone, 1992.

Tellini, G., *Il romanzo italian dell'Ottocento e Novocento*, Mondadori: Milan, 1998.

Tessari, R., *Il mito della macchina. Letteratura e industria nel primo Novocento italiano*, Mursia: Milan, 1973.; *La Scapigliatura*, Paravia: Turin, 1975.

Tietze-Conrat, E., *Dwarfs and Jesters in Art*, Plaidon: London, 1957.

Ubersfeld, A., *Le Roi et le Bouffon*, Librairie José Corti: Paris, 1973., *V. Hugo, Oeuvres Complètes*, Théâtre, I, Robert Laffont: Paris, 1985.

Walker, F., (editor), *A. Boito, Lettere inedite e poesie giovanili*, Siena, 1959.; *The Man Verdi*, Dent: London, 1962.

Welesford, E., *The Fool: His Social and Literary History*, Faber: London, 1935.

Willeford, W., *The Fool and his Sceptre*, Northwestern University Press, 1969.

Woolf, D., *The Art of Verga. A Study in Objectivity*, Sydney University Press, Sydney, 1977.

INDEX

Pirandello, Lina, 99
Pirandello, Luigi, 5, 68. *see also Il berretto a sonagli*
  deconstruction, 91
  Dualism, 120–121
  interest in insanity, 98–99
Poe, Edgar Allan, 55
poetic form
  deconstruction of, 22, 61, 111, 120
  deformity of, 119
  imagery, 75
  and music, 119
Politecnico, 68
Portinari, Folco, 20
Portulano, Antoinetta, 98
Praga, Emilio, 29, 43, 48
prayer
  Otello, 71–73, 76, 84
psychological states
  Il berretto a sonagli, 98
  Mefistofeles, 67–68
  Otello, 77–82, 120
  Rigoletto, 4, 10, 13–18
Puccini, G.A., 62
puppet, image of, 120
  Il berretto a sonagli, 99–121
  Le roi s'amuse, 7
  symbolism, 4, 106–8, 110

Q
Quadrelli, Rodolfo, 29, 48

R
Rabelais, F., 5
Re Orso (Boito), 61, 91
  analysis of, 48–55
  Art as victim, 96
  concept of self, 68
  Dualism, 70
  poetic convention, 91–92, 119, 120
realism, 1–2
  and Romanticism, 2–3, 13, 19, 48, 80

ugliness, 29–30
Reason, 120–121
Il berretto a sonagli, 92, 98, 113–5
  loss of (*see* madness)
  Otello, 70
  redefinition of, 63
resurrection, 37, 40
Ricordi, Giulio, 75
Rigoletto, 3, 6, 10–11, 35, 67
  analysis of, 12–21
  fusion of genre, 91
  Good and Evil, 20–21
  key words, 17–18
  laughter and tears, 18–19
  light and dark in, 10–11
  master and servant, 95
  psychological drama, 13–15
Risorgimento, 3, 27
Romani, 68
Romanticism, 27, 45, 68.
  see also realism
  crisis of, 92

S
Salina, Count Agostino, 48
San Secondo, Rosso di, 99
Sanctis, Francesco De, 93
Scapigliatura Milanese, 3, 10, 12, 27–28, 34, 93
  Art *versus* Science, 92
  Austro-Prussian war, 48
  development of, 28–30
  Dualism, 79
  embalming, 38
  and Modernism, 85, 119
  realism, 66
Scarsi, Giovanna, 48
Scènes de la vie de Boheme (Murger), 29
Sciascia, Leonardo,102
Science, 99
  analysis of mummy, 38–40
  behavioural science, 1

STUDIES IN ITALIAN LITERATURE

1. Foscarina Alexander, **The Aspiration Toward a Lost Natural Harmony in the Work of Three Italian Writers: Leopardi, Verga, and Moravia**

2. Sharon Harwood-Gordon, **A Study of the Theology and the Imagery of Dante's** *Divina Commedia*: **Sensory Perception, Reason and Free Will**

3. Marc Cirigliano (ed. & trans.), **The Complete Lyric Poems of Dante Alighieri**

4. Mary Morrison, **The Tragedies of G.-B. Giraldi Cinthio: The Transformation of Narrative Source into Stage Play**

5. Joseph F. Privitera (English translation and critical edition), **Luigi Pirandello (1867-1936)–His Plays in Sicilian** (2 volumes)

6. Anthony Julian Tamburri, **A Reconsideration of Aldo Palazzeschi's Poetry (1905-1974): Revisiting the** *Saltimbanco*

7. Lynne Press and Pamela Williams, **Women and Feminine Images in Giacomo Leopardi, 1798-1837: Bicentenary Essays**

8. Simon A. Gilson, **Medieval Optics and Theories of Light in the Works of Dante**

9. C.E.J. Griffiths, **The Theatrical Works of Govacchino Forzano–Drama for Mussolini's Italy,** and in an appendix, **Racconti d'autunno, d'inverno e di primavera** by Giovacchino Forzano

10. Deirdre O'Grady, **Piave, Boito, Pirandello–From Romantic Realism to Modernism**

11. Joseph F. Privitera, **A Reference Grammar of Medieval Italian, According to Dante, with a Dual Edition of the** *Vita Nova*